GREECE
UNDER
THE JUNTA

GREECE UNDER THE JUNTA

Edited by

Peter Schwab
Dept. of Political Studies
Adelphi University (Garden City, N. Y.)

and

George D. Frangos
Dept. of History
Columbia University (New York, N. Y.)

FACTS ON FILE   NEW YORK

GREECE UNDER THE JUNTA

Library of Congress Catalog Card No. 77-117973

ISBN 0-87196-177-6

9 8 7 6 5 4 3 2 1

PRINTED IN THE UNITED STATES OF AMERICA

CONTENTS

•

ILLUSTRATIONS

INTRODUCTION

A MILITARY JUNTA FORMED by a group of right-wing army colonels seized control of Greece Apr. 21, 1967. This *coup d'etat,* the 5th by the armed forces since the 1920s, ended a long-standing political crisis but ushered in a new period of political strife. Following the coup, opposition leaders were imprisoned, the junta was accused of barbarously torturing political prisoners, and underground resistance groups were created to fight the military regime. The king of Greece failed in an attempted counter-coup and then went into exile.

The *coup d'etat* took place during a period of political disharmony such as is virtually traditional in Greece.

In its 140 years of independence, modern Greece has been a scene of turmoil and political instability. During this relatively brief period, as for centuries previously, Greece's strategic position in the Eastern Mediterranean and on the southeastern flank of Europe has attracted the attention and interest of the world's powers. This situation was recognized by the U.S. after World War II when, in 1947, it announced its first major military and economic commitment, the Truman Doctrine, in support of its policy of containment of Soviet expansion. President Harry S. Truman called for an initial expenditure of $400 million in military and economic aid to Greece and Turkey to help insure that they remained part of the Western world.

Foreign intervention, *coups d'etat* and war have been common in the history of modern Greece. A nation of nearly 9 million people, Greece was established as a modern state in 1830 after an 8-year war of independence (1821-9) against

the Ottoman Empire. Britain, France and Russia decided at that time that Greece would become a monarchy governed by a prince of their selection, and they promised to protect and guarantee its independence. In 1833 Prince Otto of Bavaria was selected to become King Othon of Greece. He ruled until 1862, when his dynasty was overthrown and he was expelled. In 1863 Othon was replaced by a Danish Prince whose dynasty (Gluksberg) reigned, with some interruptions, and is still officially the ruling family.

During World War I the monarchy became the center of a controversy that has yet to be resolved: Eleutherios Venizelos, a pro-republican premier, opposed King Constantine I's policy of neutrality in World War I. The king was deposed after French and British troops landed in Greece in 1917. After the war the king returned, only to be deposed again in 1922 by a military coup after a disastrous defeat in a war with Turkey.

A republic was established in 1923. Military coups were executed in 1925, 1926, 1933 and 1935. The coup of 1926 established a military dictator, Gen. Theodore Pangalos, who became famous for his decree forbidding women to wear skirts more than 14 inches above the ground.

The monarchy was reestablished in 1935 under King George II. The following year, on Aug. 4, 1936, Gen. John Metaxas established a fascist dictatorship that lasted until his death in 1941, the year Greece entered World War II. King George remained head of state throughout the Metaxas and wartime periods, although he spent the war years in exile.

During the years of Nazi occupation one of the most powerful resistance movements in occupied Europe developed in Greece under the leadership of the Greek Communist Party. The rank and file of the National Liberation Front (EAM/ELLAS), however, were primarily non-Communist. When Nazi forces withdrew in 1944, EAM/ELLAS held virtual control of the entire country. In accordance with an agreement between British Prime Min. Winston Churchill and Soviet Communist Party Secy. Joseph Stalin, which assigned Greece to a British sphere of responsibility, Britain landed troops in Athens to insure the establishment of the Greek government, which had been in exile in the Middle East during World War II. Hostilities erupted in Dec. 1944 when the Communist-led resistance forces refused to comply with British demands to disarm. A truce was established in Jan. 1945, but civil war broke out again in 1947 and continued until the Communist forces were defeated in 1949.

Reconstruction and recovery, with U.S. aid, took place throughout the 1950s, especially under the conservative National Radical Union (ERE), led by Premier Constantine Karamanlis. The monarchy, which had been returned from its wartime exile in 1947, played, according to many observers, an important role in supporting Greek conservative forces. (King George II died in 1947, and his brother, Paul I, became king.) Premier Karamanlis resigned June 11, 1963, after 8 years in power, because of a clash with the monarchy. After several months of rule by a caretaker government (led by Panayotis Pipinelis of ERE), the Center Union party, led by George Papandreou, won the election of Nov. 3, 1963. The new government announced the release of all political prisoners who had been detained since the end of the civil war.

In July 1965 King Constantine II, who had ascended the throne on the death of his father, King Paul, Mar. 6, 1964, clashed with Premier Papandreou over allegations that a leftist organization known as *Aspida* (the Shield) had penetrated the army. Defense Min. Petros Garoufalias refused to resign, as Papandreou demanded, and the king dismissed Papandreou July 15 as premier. A new Center Union government was then formed by George Athanasiadis-Novas, the speaker of the Greek parliament. Commenting on the clash between the king and Papandreou, the London *Times'* correspondent reported in a July 4 dispatch that Constantine was "strongly opposed to any changes in the army which might expose it to Communist penetration" whereas Papandreou was "under pressure from his [Center Union] party to rid the army of right-wing officers whose loyalty to his administration is questioned."

Before Papandreou's ouster, a report on the disciplinary aspects of the *Aspida* case had been published by Gen. Ioannis Simos, chief of the Military Justice Department; Papandreou's Center Union government June 8 had then ordered a judicial investigation of the matter. In his report Simos expressed the opinion that *Aspida* was founded and directed by 14 "vain and excited officers" for the purpose of "seeking personal benefits such as favorable transfers and appointments, missions abroad, etc., by promoting initiated officers to important or key army posts." The report emphasized the activities of a captain who had boasted of having personal contacts with the premier and his son, Andreas Papandreou, deputy economic coordination minister. Opposition parties and newspapers had charged, after Simos had published his report, that the Papandreou government was trying to suppress the *Aspida* affair. The opposition newspapers asserted that although the existence of the organization had been disclosed by the government in March, no action had been taken for more than 2 months. According to opposition newspapers, several members of the Papandreou government had been named during Simos' inquiry as having had contacts with *Aspida* conspirators.

After Defense Min. Garoufalias refused Papandreou's demand that he resign, the cabinet July 12 decided to expel him from the government. Garoufalias ignored this decision and held that "no one can expel me from the camp to which I have adhered." It was reported that the king had refused to sign a decree, submitted by George Papandreou, under which Garoufalias would have been dismissed and the Defense Ministry turned over to Papandreou himself. Papandreou then told Constantine July 15 that he would resign July 16, but the king was said to have replied that he was accepting his resignation immediately.

Following Papandreou's dismissal, massive demonstrations in support of him took place July 18 in Heraklion (Crete) and July 19 in Athens, where about 180,000 people cheered Papandreou. Police July 21 used armored cars, tear gas and hoses to disperse 30,000 pro-Papandreou demonstrators in Athens. The disorders, which began as a student demonstration outside the University of Athens, resulted in violent clashes in which a student was killed and many people, including policemen, were injured.

Athanasiadis-Novas was able to form a government only because many Center Union deputies defected from Papandreou's cause. Athanasiadis-Novas' government resigned Aug. 5, 1965 when it failed to obtain a vote of confidence from parliament. The resignation took place after 3 days of violence and demonstrations outside parliament in support of George Papandreou.

From Aug. 5, 1965 to Apr. 21, 1967 4 caretaker governments periodically ruled Greece, and a reshuffling of cabinets took place constantly. This political instability was heightened by the court-martial of the *Aspida* suspects, which began in 1966 and resulted in the conviction of 15 officers.

A 475-page indictment of alleged *Aspida* plotters, published Oct. 2, 1966, had accused 28 army officers, including 4 colonels, of "conspiring to commit acts of high treason." The officers, who were put on trial by a military court, were charged with forming a secret organization aimed at seizing power, deposing the monarchy and establishing a "different regime." The defendants were accused of having pledged to give their lives for "the establishment of democracy in the sense of rule by the most worthy, even if this should require violent procedures." Andreas Papandreou, son of George Papandreou, was alleged in the indictment to have been the political leader of *Aspida*. George Papandreou was accused of having known of his son's activities and of having destroyed, while he was premier, evidence incriminating Andreas Papandreou. The indictment was based on an inquiry in which 645 witnesses had been questioned over a 15-month period. One witness had testified that *Aspida* had planned to seize power in July 1965 to install Andreas Papandreou as premier and to hold King Constantine prisoner "until the reactions of the Americans became known."

The trial opened in Athens Nov. 14, 1966 before a court-martial made up of 4 generals with a Supreme Court senior judge as president. (Andreas Papandreou and other civilians accused in the indictment could not be tried by this military tribunal because, as civilians, they were outside its jurisdiction.) The trial ended Mar. 16, 1967 after most of the defendants had refused to defend themselves on the ground that the whole *Aspida* accusation was a "frame-up." 40 defense lawyers had boycotted the trial.

Of the 28 officers tried, 15 were convicted and 13 acquitted. Among the sentences imposed on those convicted: 18 years' imprisonment for Col. Alexandros Papaterpos, deputy director of the Central Intelligence Agency under Papandreou and the alleged leader of the *Aspida* conspiracy; 18 years for Lt. Col. Aristides Damvounellis, ex-Greek intelligence chief in Cyprus; 8 years for a lieutenant colonel; sentences of from 2 to 18 years for 12 captains, some of whom were called "instigators of the conspiracy."

In an article published Mar. 9, 1967, Andreas Papandreou asserted that forces within Greece were plotting either to rig elections scheduled for May 28 or to prevent them from being held by imposing a dictatorship. He declared that the dictatorship was being planned by a "junta whose tentacles spread from the palace to foreign intelligence services, the extreme right and the economic oligarchy." Papandreou asserted that this plot had been concocted because of a widespread belief held throughout Greece that George Papandreou's party would win the May elections, that consequently Papandreou would again be chosen as premier and that this would be seen as a personal defeat for King Constantine.

The *Athens News* reported Apr. 20, 1967 that a note sent by U.S. Pres. Lyndon B. Johnson to King Constantine was said to "have warned that the United States would in no way 'cover up' a possible dictatorship in Greece." The military coup ousting the caretaker government of Premier Panayotis Kanellopoulos took place the next day, Apr. 21. It brought to a climax the political crisis that had begun in July 1965.

COLONELS SEIZE GREECE

Government Toppled in Bloodless Coup

The interim government of Panayotis Kanellopoulos was overthrown by a military *coup d'etat* Apr. 21, 1967.

The coup was engineered by an army junta which acted early that morning. Tanks, armored cars and American-built M-59 troop carriers, which, according to informed sources, had been stationed at the Army Tank Training School in the Athens suburb of Goudi, secured strategic positions in and around Athens. It was reported that by 2:00 a.m. most government buildings had been occupied. They included the National Broadcasting Institute and the National Telecommunications Organization. By 3:00 a.m. the capital city had been secured. The country's borders were sealed, and the Athens international airport at Hellinikon was under the army's control. (It was reported later that the colonels who formed the junta had used a NATO contingency plan, "Operation Prometheus," to execute their takeover. The plan had been developed by NATO for use in the event of a Communist invasion from Greece's northern neighbors.)

This decree, which was broadcast over the Greek radio at 6 a.m. Apr. 21 and published 2 days later, was the first official news of the change in government: "The armed forces have taken over the government of the country. The king, in accordance with Article No. 91 of the Greek constitution 'following a proposal by the cabinet, in case of serious trouble or an obvious threat to the public security and order of the country,' has ordered with a royal decree the suspension all over the country of Articles No. 5, 6, 8, 10, 11,

13

12, 14, 20, 95, and 97 of the constitution. The king also in accordance with Article No. 91 has formed special courts-martial."

A curfew was declared. (But it was lifted partially after 72 hours and totally within a week.) Vehicles and pedestrians were banned from the streets. Banks and the stock exchange were closed. Food or goods hoarding, it was announced, would be considered "sabotage" and would be punishable by court-martial.

It was announced Apr. 21 that the country was considered in a "state of siege" under terms of a law passed in 1912. (This condition remained in effect when this book went to press 3 years later.) The state-of-siege rules stipulated that: "(1) Individuals can be apprehended and arrested without charge. They can be detained for any length of time. (2) There is no bail for political crimes. (3) All citizens, independent of position, can be brought before an emergency court-martial (4) All gatherings, indoors or outdoors, are forbidden. All gatherings will be dissolved by force. (5) It is forbidden to form a syndicate [union] or group with labor union aims. Strikes are completely forbidden. (6) It is permitted to search houses, political premises, public buildings, all buildings, day and night, without special warrant. (7) It is forbidden to announce or publish any kind of information in any way through the press, radio and television without censorship beforehand. (8) Letters, telegrams and all means of communication will be censored. (9) Crimes, political crimes as well as those of the press, whether they have to do with private life or not, as well as the crimes to be judged by the court of appeal, will be judged by court-martial. (10) Everyone who commits a crime which should be punished by law, even if it is not against the army, will also be judged by court-martial."

More specific prohibitions were announced Apr. 25 by Lt. Gen. Odysseus Anghelis, army chief of staff: "In conformity with the law concerning siege and Royal Decree No. 280 the following are prohibited: Open air gatherings of more than 5 persons, indoor gatherings of the same number, the bearing of arms, temporary hospitality given at home to persons not belonging to one's family without police permission [which must be secured within 2 hours]. . . ."

Army patrols reportedly arrested between 2,500 and 6,000 persons within the first 48 hours of the coup. They included most of the country's major political leaders as well as individuals thought to be leftist or Communist. Among those arrested early the morning of the coup were: Kanellopoulos, ex-Premiers George Papandreou (Center Union leader) and Stefanos Stefanopoulos (National Radical Union, or ERE); Andreas Papandreou; Maj. Michael Arnaoutis, King Constantine's personal secretary; Alexander Papaligouras, ERE defense minister; Constantine Mitsotakis, a Liberal Party deputy; Nicholas Bacopoulos, Center Union house leader; Ioannis Passaliades, head of EDA (United Democratic Left), the leftist and pro-national Communist party.

The more prominent political leaders were confined in several hotels in Athens. Other prisoners were taken to detention camps that were hastily established. At least 2 soccer stadiums were converted for this purpose. All jails and many local police stations were filled with political prisoners. Several days later many were transferred to the Greek prison islands Leros, Yioura and Agios Efstratios in the Aegean Sea.

5 of Athens' 14 daily newspapers were shut down permanently. The remaining 9 were subjected to censorship and were required to carry official news and proclamations. Many magazines and journals also ceased publication. These included those allegedly controlled or sympathetic to leftist parties and ideas.

Government Formed, Coup's Aim Explained

The leaders of the coup made themselves known the evening of Apr. 21 as they announced the formation of a new government. The following leaders of the coup, some taking

Leaders of the junta, first row (left to right): Nikolaos Markarezos, George Papadopoulos and Stylianos Pattakos

subsidiary positions in the Council of Ministers (cabinet), were then reported to be the junta's most powerful figures: Col. George Papadopoulos — minister to the premier; Brig. Gen. Stylianos Pattakos — interior and security minister; Lt. Gen. Gregory E. Spandidakis — deputy premier and defense minister; Col. Nikolaos Makarezos — economic coordination minister.

An ex-Supreme Court chief prosecutor, Constantine V. Kollias, was appointed premier; he was the only high-ranking civilian in the cabinet. Other ministers, appointed as of Apr. 22, included: *Foreign Affairs*— Pavlos Economu-Gouras; *Finance*— Adamantios Androutsopoulos; *Education*— Constantine Kalabocas; *Justice*— Leonidas Rozakis; *Public Works*— Panayotis Tsarouhis; *Agriculture*— Alexander Matthaiou; *Communications*— Dimitrios Economopoulos; *Trade*— George Papadimitracopoulos; *Industry*— Nicholas Economopoulos; *Public Order*— Evangelos Karabetsos and then Pavlos Totomis; *Merchant Marine*— Vice Adm. Athanasios Athanasiou; *Health & Social Welfare*— Efstratios Poulatzas; *Labor*— Christos J. Apostolakos; *Undersecretary, National Defense*— Gen. George Ziotakis; *Undersecretary, Economic Coordination*— Rolandos Rodinos. 4 new ministers were appointed Apr. 26: *Communications*— I. Tsantilas; *Labor*— A. Lekkas; *Finance Undersecretary*— Spyridon Lizardos; *Commerce Undersecretary*— G. Georgakelos.

Papadopoulos, who ultimately emerged as the leader and "strongman" of the junta, had been an officer of the psychological warfare branch of the Greek army's general staff. Pattakos had been commander of the Army Tank Training School in the Athens suburb of Goudi, where the coup was initiated. Makarezos had been merely a colonel of artillery. These 3 major coup leaders and their associates were largely of lower middle-class, rural background and were considered army careerists. Many observers noted what appeared to be a class antagonism between the coup leaders and the royalists, higher-ranking army officers and other members of elite groups who had ruled Greece for generations. Both sides, however, were staunchly anti-Communist.

(A shake-up in the military was announced Apr. 23.
5 generals were retired from the army. Lt. Gen. Odysseus
Anghelis was named chief of the army staff, replacing current Deputy Premier and Defense Min. Spandidakis, who
held the post at the time of the coup. The navy chief of staff,
Vice Adm. Nicholas Engolfopoulos, was relieved of his command Apr. 26. Another announcement May 17 disclosed that
8 major generals, 17 brigadier generals and hundreds of
lower-ranking officers had been forced to retire.)

At 10 p.m. Apr. 21 the new premier addressed the nation
by radio. Delivering the new government's first official statement, Kollias described the junta's political and ideological
position and explained why it had acted. According to the
Athens daily *Eleftheros Kosmos*, Premier Kollias said:

"For a long time we have been witness to crimes which
have been committed against our society and nation. The
unhesitating and miserable exchange between [political]
parties, the deviation from the way of duty of the great part
of the press, the systematic attack against all institutions,
their corrosion, the humiliation of Parliament ... the paral-
ysis of the state machine, a decline of morals ... the secret
and open collaboration of subversive elements have all
destroyed the serenity of the country, created a climate of
anarchy and chaos and have led us to the verge of national
destruction. There has been no other means of salvation but
the intervention of our armed forces.

"This intervention naturally consists of a violation of
the constitution, but this was necessary for the salvation of
the nation. The salvation of the nation is the superior law....
All over the country absolute serenity and order prevails.
The premier and the members of the cabinet have been
mobilized for that reason.

"... We belong to no party and support no particular
faction.... We are led exclusively by patriotic motives, and
we aim at destroying depravity, to clean up public life, to
throw out of the state organization the putrification from
which it was threatened.

"After the establishment of normal life and the creation of suitable conditions in the shortest amount of time, the country will return to the parliamentarians on a healthy basis. Then the mission of the new government will be over."

A government spokesman told newsmen Apr. 26 that the immediate purpose of the coup was to prevent "a revolution that might otherwise have begun in [the northern city of] Salonika today." The government spokesman said that "only military action could have maintained order." The spokesman promised that the junta would produce evidence that a Communist insurrection had been planned and that George Papandreou, leader of the Center Union party, had conspired with the Communists to provoke a riot as he addressed his followers during a campaign speech in Salonika.

Papadopoulos said Apr. 27 that "70 3-ton trucks had been used to carry the evidence of a Communist plot that the army intervened to prevent." Papadopoulos, meeting with newsmen, said that the new government's aim "is an early return to normal parliamentary life." He reiterated that the army had acted to "save the nation from the precipice of communism." In referring to the restrictions imposed by the junta, Papadopoulos said, "Do not forget that we are before a diseased person whom we have on the operating table, and if the surgeon does not fasten him to the table during the operation, there is the possibility that, instead of restoring his health, we will lead him to death. The restrictions are only the necessary act of fastening the diseased body to the operating table."

The interior minister, Brig. Gen. Stylianos Pattakos, said Apr. 29 that the junta would present a revised constitution providing for a strong executive leader. Pattakos said that "strict discipline is necessary at present," but "there will be greater freedom of speech and expression" in the future. Discussing the proposed constitution, Pattakos said May 3 that the Greek people would be given a chance to "vote if they like the new constitution or the amendments we may make." He announced May 8 that the Council of Ministers had approved a motion providing for the establishment of a 25-member committee to study the "constitution presently in force and suggest new articles to bring it up to date." He said the committee would be composed of jurists, economists, former university rectors and other specialists. He added that the new government was planning to establish a permanent electoral system with a "tendency toward the majority voting system, and to bring about other innovations."

Pattakos said the reason for revising the constitution was to "remove certain deficiencies it had and to add new articles based on the modern constitutions of other countries." He added that "the findings of the committee would be submitted to the government which, after studying them, would decide whether to approve of the revised constitution." "If the government approved it, the new charter would be submitted to a nationwide referendum," Pattakos continued. "If the Greek people also approved it, and providing the necessary conditions existed, general elections would then be held for a return to parliamentary life."

In the first days after the coup, the junta made several policy statements in which it promised to reform Greek society and return it to the "ideals of Helleno-Christian civilization." There would be "social reforms, assistance and reformation of the church, help for workers, more assistance to mothers, aid for youth, social justice generally and love for the villages. Taxes would be reformed, economic development supported and education advanced." The Cyprus question "will be settled quickly and finally."

Pattakos Apr. 27 directed the Education Ministry to ban long hair for boys and miniskirts for girls and to order students to attend Sunday mass regularly and to avoid such entertainments as pinball machines. It was ordered that all persons must enter buses and trolleys from the rear door and exit only from the front.

The government announced May 9 that "foreign tourists having what is considered a 'beatnik' appearance will be barred from Greece." Pattakos and Public Order Min. Totomis said in a joint statement: "Foreigners with filthy and tattered clothing and wearing beards or long hair will be turned back at the border." Tourists who "do not possess the required means for their maintenance, that is $80 per person for a stay in Greece up to 10 days, will also be banned." These tourist directives, however, were repealed May 15.

King's Role in the Coup

The coup leaders said in their first announcement Apr. 21 that they had taken control of Greece with King Constantine's support. But it was reported Apr. 22 that the king had refused to sign the decree declaring martial law and suspending the constitution. Although the king had made no public pronouncement, a government spokesman, Nicholas Farmakis, reiterated the claim Apr. 23 that the king had signed the martial-law decree. When asked at a news conference to produce the decree, Farmakis said: "The government does not have to prove anything in writing."

Premier Kollias announced Apr. 24 that Constantine would preside over a meeting of the cabinet "in the course of the week." But it was also reported Apr. 24 that in talks with U.S. Amb.-to-Greece Phillips Talbot, the king maintained his resistance to the coup and sought to bring about a return to constitutional government.

Rumors of the king's early resistance to the takeover apparently were contradicted by the disclosure that he had been in attendance when the new ministers were sworn in during the evening of the day the coup took place. Photographs showing his presence were published prominently in all newspapers when they appeared the following Sunday (Apr. 24). It was widely believed, however, that the purpose of the king's presence was to use his influence to secure the inclusion of several conservative civilians, among them the man chosen as premier, Constantine Kollias, in the cabinet.

The king Apr. 26 attended a cabinet meeting of the new government in the Royal Palace. His appearance there seemed to be evidence that he did not openly oppose the army leaders. But Constantine said after the meeting that it was his "fervent wish that the country shall revert to parliamentary government as soon as possible. For myself, as king of the Hellenes, I shall do my duty toward my country and toward my people."

Col. Nikolaos Makarezos, the new regime's economic coordination minister and a leader of the coup, admitted in a May 1 UPI interview that the military had acted without the king's knowledge "because we had to protect him from those who would accuse him of being the instigator."

King Constantine noted May 21 that the junta had arranged for a committee of 20 experts to begin drafting a new constitution within a month. The work should be completed in about 6 months, the king said. "After a final elaboration of the text, the government will submit it for the ratification of the people by a plebiscite," he asserted. (The king simultaneously announced the birth May 20 of a son, Paul, heir to the throne. Constantine and his Danish-born queen, Anne-Marie, already had one daughter, Alexia.)

POST-COUP DEVELOPMENTS

Political Reform: Liberal & Leftist Groups Disbanded

The junta's political reforms began Apr. 29, when it announced that the United Democratic Left (EDA), an extreme leftist party, had been abolished. The party had received 12-1/2% of the vote in the last (1964) election. Most of the EDA leaders had been among those arrested during the early morning hours of the coup. Premier Kollias said May 3 that the government had dissolved EDA under a 1947 law outlawing the Greek Communist Party (KKE; the leaders of KKE had been in exile in Eastern Europe since the end of the Greek civil war in 1949). He said police authorities had assured him that the party was in fact a "front for the KKE." He added: "It is sufficient to point out that EDA adopted the proclamation of the 7th plenary session of the KKE, according to which the aim was to gradually detach Greece from the West . . . by methods of neutrality."

A government proclamation May 4 announced the dissolution of at least 279 liberal as well as leftist organizations. Lt. Gen. Odysseus Anghelis, Army chief of staff, ordered the confiscation of the groups' assets and records. About 3/4 of the banned groups were labor unions; the rest were various youth, student, athletic, civic improvement and women's organizations. Among the groups banned were: the Lambrakis Youth Organization (associated with EDA), the Bertrand Russell Association and the Union of Greek Democratic Jurists.

It was announced May 5 that the youth organizations of all political parties, including that of the conservative ERE, had been ordered to disband. Premier Kollias said that the reason for the disbanding of the youth groups was that "they were abandoning their education and, instead of being educated to become good citizens, they were educating themselves in mob-rule and sidewalk demonstrations. It was time that [youths] returned to their task and to the way of virtue and duty."

Pattakos announced May 6 that the cabinet had decided to abolish the constitutional provisions for the free election of municipal and communal (village) officials. He said that in the future, such officials would be appointed by the interior minister or local prefect. (Prefects are government-appointed executives who head each of Greece's provinces.)

The junta May 6 ordered the disbanding of all municipal and village councils (composed of mayors and village presidents within each of Greece's 52 provinces). Each prefect was asked to prepare a list of approved candidates to be chosen by the government to replace "those municipal and communal leaders who had been incompetent."

Pattakos announced May 19 that the junta had dismissed more than half of Greece's prefects under a May 18 decree ending the term of office of every active prefect. The only prefects retained were those who had received "top marks by the government." 20 such prefects were reappointed. 23 other prefects were dismissed, and their replacements were chosen and sworn in May 22.

Administration & Education

The junta Apr. 26 announced a plan for the reorganization of government administration. Interior Min. Pattakos called on all civil servants to recognize that "their mission is the loyal service of the legal interests of the citizens." "It is indisputable that the civil servants are responsible for certain imperfections of the Greek citizen,"

Pattakos asserted. "Nepotism, corruption and demogoguery must be purged from government."

The government May 3 announced "the abolition of bureaucracy." Premier Kollias made public a cabinet decision that prescribed "the obligation of all civil servants to defend their actions on application by citizens, within 3 days for simple cases and 7 days for more complicated affairs. Intervention by 3d parties, influence peddlers and contact men in government is prohibited."

Kollias May 9 said the government had drafted 3 decrees aimed at "restoring sound functioning of civil services." These decrees provided for the termination of term in office of "all special advisers and senior officials of state organizations...as well as for the abolition of certain provisions which are opposed to the common sentiment of justice and morality." These provisions included civil-service job security. The decrees also required all public servants, including public and private teachers, to sign a loyalty oath. The draft decrees were officially enacted in July and August. Terms of the decrees, as translated from *Efimerida tis Kyverniseos* (the official government gazette):

"Civil servants...are formally dismissed...if their disloyalty is established; the provisions of the constitution concerning irremovability and all those protecting labor agreements are suspended in the cases referred to." [Basic Decree No. 9, Article 1]

"The following are considered to be disloyal: the official, employe, worker and assistant who is imbued with Communist or anti-national ideas, or who makes propaganda in their favor, or contributes in any way to their dissemination, or praises them, or has any form of contact or relations with the holders of these opinions...or takes part in sedition or in a public open-air meeting that has been forbidden or during which anti-national or Communist slogans are uttered...." [Basic Decree No. 9, Article 2]

The junta's strongman: Col. George Papadopoulos

"For the purposes of verification of their loyalty, all the civil servants referred to above must submit to the responsible minister...a written declaration of their loyalty...." [Basic Decree No. 9, Article 3]

The first action in the field of education was taken May 7 when the government announced its decision to give all technical text books free to needy high school students. The junta simultaneously declared that "the state will publish text books, and authorship royalties will be paid to the professors after an assessment is made by a special committee which will be established." Previously, text books had been sold to students directly by their professors, who were also the books' authors. Interior Min. Pattakos said May 8 that free text books would be given to all students regardless of need. He added that entrance to all Greek universities would be free and that no charges would be levied on students when they applied for university entrance examinations.

A government decree June 21 ordered that 10% of candidates to institutions of higher learning beginning in the academic year 1967-8 were to be admitted "solely on the grounds of high moral character and reproachless behavior." A special committee was to be established and appointed by the government to select these students. It was ordered Sept. 5, under Decree No. 129, that, from the 4th year of primary schooling, *Katharevousa* (an artificial literary language closely resembling ancient Greek) would be used for all oral and written school work. Under the same law, compulsory education was cut from 9 years to 6.

Junta's Initial Economic Actions

George Papadopoulos, minister to the premier, told newsmen Apr. 28 that the aim of the new government was "the economic development of the country within the framework of the European Economic Community."

Col. Nikolaos Makarezos, minister of economic coordination, discussing the regime's economic policies, said May 11 that "the government will stress faith in the principle that the individual is both free as a producer and as a consumer; but this is on the basis of legal increases of his financial benefits. We reject any deviation from the theory of free business initiative. The state's role is restricted to the safeguarding of national security, without which no business can carry on."

Makarezos said May 23 that the state "attributes particular importance to the influx of foreign capital. What interests us is the application of a development policy and not the conversion of the country into a testing ground for theories."

Interior Min. Pattakos announced Apr. 26 that the dismissal of laborers and employes was prohibited and that employers must pay salaries, wages and Easter bonuses (1/2 of one month's pay) in full. Infringements of this order would be referred to courts-martial, Pattakos warned. He directed May 1 that municipal land be distributed among landless farmers. He again instructed all employers to pay their workers Easter bonuses without delay.

The government announced May 10 that "no price increase will be allowed for any kind of commodity" and that all goods must continue being sold at pre-Apr. 21 prices.

Economic Coordination Min. Makarezos announced May 15 that Litton Industries, Inc. of Beverly Hills, Calif. had agreed to participate in a 12-year program aimed at developing Crete and the western Peloponnesus. Litton would provide consultants, advise and promote the $828 million investment scheme. (Negotiations between Litton and the pre-coup government had fallen through and had been terminated.)

Agriculture Min. Alexandros Mattheou said May 27 that the government planned a land reform program that would enable large farmers to purchase smaller holdings. Small farmers would be encouraged to find jobs in rural industries to be stimulated by the government.

Junta Dissolves Synod, Picks New Archbishop

The reorganization of the Greek Church began May 9 when Premier Kollias announced a decree that dissolved the 12-member Holy Synod (the ruling body of the church). A new 9-member synod was appointed by the junta. Archbishop Chrysostomos, 87, head of the Greek Church, was forced to resign May 11 after the government had decreed May 10 that all bishops must retire by the age of 80. The new synod was asked to nominate 3 candidates from whom the government would choose the new leader of the church.

Archimandrite Ieronymos Kotsonis, 61, was selected by the junta May 13 as archbishop of Athens and primate of the Greek Orthodox Church in Greece. (The patriarch of Constantinople, Athenagoras, is the theoretical head of all Orthodox Churches. The Church of Greece has been autonomous since 1850.) Before his appointment, Kotsonis had been palace chaplain and the king's personal confessor for 18 years. He had also been a professor of canon law at the University of Salonika.

In his enthronement speech May 17 the new archbishop called for a "fundamental change in the spirit of the church." He said that payments by the faithful to clergy for christenings, weddings and funerals would be suppressed. The church would reorganize its finances over a period of 10 years to become independent of state grants, Kotsonis declared. He promised reforms in religious education, church recruitment and administrative organization.

(The regime announced Feb. 17, 1969 that it had granted the Greek Orthodox Church a new charter. The new charter gave the church the right to adopt its own rules, manage its financial resources, train and appoint clerics and control its own agencies and institutions. It also called for the formation of a general church assembly composed of all bishops and heads of church organizations and one layman from each diocese. Local clergy-laity councils were to be introduced in all dioceses and were expected to limit the powers of local bishops. The granting of the charter was hailed by the junta as a step in establishing the church's independence from state control. Clerical critics of the new charter, however, pointed to provisions that allow the government to retain its right to name bishops and maintain control in the appointment of members to the newly created assembly and local councils.)

NATO Allies Condemn Coup

Notes condemning the coup were circulated by representatives of Denmark and Norway May 5 among NATO defense ministers meeting in Paris. The Danish statement expressed the hope that the military government would be "of short duration" and that political prisoners would be freed quickly. The Norwegian statement charged that the coup was "a flagrant violation of the principles of parliamentarian democracy."

The Greek representative to NATO, Christian Xanthopoulos-Palamas, in a letter to NATO Secy. Gen. Manlio Brosio May 6, assailed the Danish/Norwegian statements as "unacceptable interference in the domestic affairs of a member state." A Danish government proposal that the notes be discussed and debated by the NATO conference members was rejected by Brosio after consultations with the Danish representative Henning Hjorth-Nielsen. The Greek representative said, in regard to the Danish proposal, that "I am obliged to lodge the strongest protest against this unfortunate action."

The Greek Foreign Ministry May 16 lodged a protest with the Danish government over demonstrations in Copenhagen against the military regime in Greece. The Greek note said: "The Greek government considers that the recent demonstrations which occurred in Denmark, following the latest political change in Greece, constitute an unacceptable attempt at intervention in purely domestic affairs of this country.... Greece is being defamed by inaccuracies and malignant accusations which are being fabricated at the centers of international communism."

Following continued criticism of the new regime in several official and private quarters in Western Europe, the Greek government stated May 12 that it was "following with great sadness the stand of certain foreign newspapers and labor organizations which, in ignorance of exactly what happened in Greece, are looking at events through the eyes of special interests.... It should not be forgotten that [present-day Greeks] are the same people of 3,000 years ago who taught the world what democracy was. They are those who defended Western civilization since the dawn of its history, against the Asian aggressors of antiquity and the fascists, Nazis and Communists of modern times."

U.S. & British Response to Coup

The first high-level U.S. comment on the Greek military coup had been made in Washington Apr. 28 by State Secy. Dean Rusk. Rusk had said that the U.S. was "awaiting concrete evidence that the new Greek government will make every effort to re-establish democratic institutions which have been an integral part of Greek political life."

Rusk told the U.S. House Foreign Affairs Committee May 4 that the U.S. did not intend to intervene in Greece and, "except for our continuous moral support of King Constantine, there is nothing else we can do."

Defense Secy. Robert S. McNamara said May 11 that he had told Greek Deputy Premier and National Defense Min. Gregorios E. Spandidakis that the U.S. might curtail military aid to Greece, unless the new regime restored constitutional rule. Returning from the NATO conference, McNamara said he had expressed to Spandidakis the U.S.' disappointment with "the move away from democracy, from constitutional government, in Greece." The State Department announced May 16 that "major items" of U.S. military equipment scheduled for shipment to Greece had been withheld during recent weeks. Officials said the measure was a "selective embargo" imposed to pressure the Athens regime to curb military rule. (According to press reports, U.S. military aid to Greece had totaled $1.3 billion since 1950. It amounted to $78.7 million in fiscal 1966.)

Spandidakis had said in a press interview May 5 that "there is no indication that the U.S. will stop its military aid to Greece.... Our faith in NATO remains as strong as ever." But Greek Coordination Min. Nicholas Makarezos had warned the U.S. May 5 that it would have to maintain aid shipments if it "wants Greece to stay outside the Iron Curtain."

After the U.S. had imposed its "selective embargo," Greek Interior Min. Stylianos Pattakos said May 16 that Greece would not look elsewhere for military assistance despite the U.S. action.

British Foreign Secy. George Brown told the British Labor Party conference Oct. 4 that the British government wanted "to see a return to legal and constitutional government" but that such a return would be easier if Britain maintained its contacts with the military regime. He said that it was easy "to talk about expelling Greece from here or there" but that, if such action were to end "in murder and bloodshed that we could not affect," Britain would be held responsible.

A resolution expressing indignation over the "seizure of power by the Greek military clique" was adopted by 3,167,000 — 2,898,000 vote of the Labor Party conference Oct. 4. The resolution called for (a) the explusion of Greece from the North Atlantic Alliance, (b) the discontinuance of all military aid to Greece and (c) the severance of Greece's association with such European organizations as the Common Market and the Council of Europe until "the military dictatorship gives way to viable and proper democracy." It also (d) urged the British Labor government to raise the issue of Greece in the UN, (e) called on the Greek government to release all political prisoners and hold free elections and (f) declared support for "all actions taken by the Greek working class to bring down the regime." (Brown had asked the delegates to remit the resolution to the Labor Party National Executive.)

Communist Relations with Greece

Addressing a conference of leaders of 24 European Communist parties at Karlovy Vary, Czechoslovakia Apr. 24, Soviet Communist Party Gen. Secy. Leonid I. Brezhnev branded the Greek coup as an attempt to "establish a fascist dictatorship."

The Greek Foreign Ministry May 21 accused the European Communist states of intervening in Greece's domestic affairs by allowing demonstrations against Greek embassies and "hypocritically" protesting the suspension of constitutional rights in Greece. But Premier Kollias said May 23 that the anxieties of East European Communist governments were "unjustified in regard to the effects that the change in Greece might have on relations with them." He asserted that the junta "is willing to maintain and promote relations with all countries without exception and irrespective of different political and social systems."

(The Greek government had announced May 15 that it was abrogating its frontier agreement with Yugoslavia, effective Nov. 13. The treaty, signed in 1959, permitted citizens of the 2 countries living in the border area to have free movement across the border.)

Political Prisoners

Interior Min. Pattakos asserted May 5 that "dangerous Communists" who had been held as political prisoners since the coup "will be released only when they become Greeks and cease obeying orders of international communism... and cease plotting against Greece." "Despite the arrest of most of them during the coup," he added, "the illegal machinery was still acting, mainly in the Athens area. Distribution of anti-government leaflets has been observed and Communist slogans have been written on walls.... The government does not accept illegalities of this kind, and it has decided, with the obvious support of all Greeks, to neutralize any infringer of the law."

Widespread reports appearing after the coup alleged that the new regime was weighing punitive action against 3 of its leading political prisoners — Communist leader Manolis Glezos, ex-Premier George Papandreou and his son, Andreas Papandreou. The reports, which said that Glezos and the younger Papandreou were in danger of execution, brought intercession on behalf of the prisoners by the UN, the Soviet Union and the U.S.

Moscow radio Apr. 28 broadcast warnings that "those who arrested Glezos and committed arbitrary action against him are preparing to take his life on the morning of Apr. 28." The Yugoslav press agency Tanyug concurred with this report. Soviet Foreign Min. Andrei Gromyko told the Greek embassy in Moscow Apr. 28 that "any attempt to do away with Manolis Glezos and any action endangering his life would arouse the indignation of the Soviet people." But a Greek government spokesman said Apr. 28 that it was "completely inaccurate" to charge that Glezos had been sentenced to death. The spokesman said that all trials resulting from the coup would be held in public.

To dispel the reports about the fate of the Papandreous, foreign newsmen were permitted to visit the father at an army hospital Apr. 28 and to visit the son at a hotel near Athens May 9. The elder Papandreou, leader of the leftist Center Union, was ordered released from military detention May 9 but was to remain under guard at his home.

John K. Galbraith, an economist and former U.S. ambassador to India, announced May 7 that Pres. Lyndon Johnson had asked the State Department "to make some representation" to the Greek government on behalf of Andreas Papandreou. Galbraith said that he had asked Mr.

Johnson to intercede. Papandreou, a former U.S. citizen and economics professor at several American universities, "was very popular" in the U.S. academic community, Galbraith said.

UN Secy. Gen. U Thant had made a personal appeal to the Greek government Apr. 29 "on humanitarian grounds on behalf of the political detainees." Thant mentioned Manolis Glezos in his appeal. After speaking with Greek Amb.-to-UN Alexis S. Liatis, Thant announced May 3 that he had been assured that prisoners in Greece would be dealt with according to "due legal judicial processes of democratic countries."

A 3-man delegation of European Socialists, representing the Socialist International, arrived in Greece May 22 to intercede for political prisoners. The delegation's leader, Bruno Pitterman of the Austrian Socialist Party, said May 23 that he was unable to negotiate for the release of any prisoners.

Pattakos announced May 9 that about half of the political prisoners detained on the island of Yioura would be released after they signed a declaration promising to abstain from any future political activity. Athens newspapers May 14 listed by name about 2,500 persons known to be held by the government.

Public Order Min. Pavlos Totomis announced May 16 that 250 detainees at Yioura had been released. He said that they were "mainly sick and aged persons" who were found free of any recent Communist activity. He repeated the government's promise that more detainees would be released "on the condition that they will undertake no future activity against the nation."

(Police May 27 arrested 2 more political leaders and closed the headquarters of the right-wing National Unity Party. Those arrested were John Tsuderos, a former member of the Center Union, and ex-Justice Min. Constantine Stefanakis.)

Underground Resistance Begins

It was reported in Paris May 12 that, according to anti-junta Greeks in exile in Western Europe, at least 2 underground resistance organizations had been formed in Greece since the coup. The first, allegedly organized by the music composer and former leftist EDA Parliament Deputy Mikis Theodorakis, was established a few days after the coup. It was named *Patriotiko Metopo* (Patriotic Front) and was said to have been responsible for distributing anti-government leaflets. The other organization, *Demokratiki Amyna* (Democratic Defense), was said to be composed mainly of Center Union and Papandreou supporters.

(Theodorakis himself was arrested and imprisoned without trial. Released at the end of Jan. 1968, Theodorakis was rearrested in Apr. 1968 and banished to the remote mountain village of Zatouna. The London *Sunday Times* Mar. 16, 1969 published a letter smuggled from Theodorakis to UN Secy. Gen. U Thant. In the letter, Theodorakis complained that he was "suffering daily from all kinds of pressures." In mid-Oct. 1969 Theodorakis was transferred from Zatouna to a military prison at Oropos, 37 miles north of Athens. He was said to be ill with diabetes and tuberculosis.)

Police in Piraeus arrested 5 persons May 6, 1967 for writing anti-government slogans on walls in the Athens suburb of Nikea. Those arrested were all under 21. Government spokesmen said that action had also been taken against the former deputy mayor of Piraeus, Nikea C. Koutouroglou, 41, who has been accused of being the leader of the 5 arrested men.

WAR OVER CYPRUS AVOIDED

Cyprus Clash Poses Greek-Turkish War Threat

War between Greece and Turkey was narrowly averted in Nov. 1967.

A communal clash on the island of Cyprus Nov. 15-16 threatened to precipitate war between Greece and Turkey. Following the clash, the Ankara government warned Greece that its forces would invade Cyprus to protect the Turkish Cypriot minority there unless Greece withdrew its troops from the island. Turkey backed its threat by mobilizing army, air and naval units and massing forces at the Turkish port of Mersin, 80 miles north of Cyprus.

International efforts to head off Greek-Turkish hostilities were undertaken by a special U.S. envoy, by the UN and by NATO, of which both Greece and Turkey are members.

The communal fighting erupted Nov. 15 in the southern villages of Ayios Theodoros (mixed population) and Kophinou (all Turkish). It caused the death of 24 Turkish Cypriots and 4 Greek Cypriots. The first clash took place when a force of Greek Cypriot police led by National Guardsmen attempted to resume patrolling the Turkish area of Ayios Theodoros, where a patrol had entered Nov. 14 but had been warned by Turkish Cypriots not to return. On approaching the village Nov. 15, the patrol was stopped by a tractor on the road and was fired on when it tried to remove it. The Greek Cypriot force returned the fire. The fighting quickly spread to neighboring Kophinou, 2 miles away, where another Greek Cypriot patrol was fired on. The violence ended early Nov. 16.

A communique issued by the Cypriot government Nov. 15 said the National Guard had "neutralized all resistance" in both villages.

A statement by the Turkish Cypriot community Nov. 16 charged that (a) the attack on Ayios Theodoros and Kophinou was an all-out military operation involving 3,000 Greek Cypriot troops, 40 armored vehicles and heavy artillery, and (b) the Greek Cypriots had fired indiscriminately on the inhabitants of the villages and had broken into homes, where they looted "everything they found in a frenzy of hatred."

Turkey's first reaction to the crisis came Nov. 16 when it warned the U.S., Britain and the UN that it would intervene militarily unless the shooting stopped at Ayios Theodoros and Kophinou. The Ankara regime alerted its air and ground forces, and Turkish naval units sailed for Mediterranean waters off Turkey's southern coast. Turkey Nov. 17 started air force reconnaissance flights over Cyprus.

Turkey was reported to have called on Greece Nov. 17 to remove its troops from Cyprus. A note delivered to Athens was said to have included these other demands: removal from Cyprus of Gen. George Grivas, commander of the Cyprus National Guard and of the Greek troops on the island (Grivas left for Athens Nov. 19 for consultation with Greek government officials and did not return to Cyprus); compensation for the deaths and damage in Ayios Theodoros; a guarantee that similar incidents would not recur; the lifting of restrictions against Turkish Cypriots currently confined to their communal enclaves.

(An estimated 8,000 to 12,000 Greek soldiers were stationed on Cyprus although only 950 were authorized under the 1960 London and Zurich agreements guaranteeing Cyprus' independence. Turkey had several hundred more troops in Cyprus than the 650 permitted. Under the 1960 Cyprus independence agreement, Britain, Greece and Turkey had the right to intervene in Cyprus if the terms of independence were not kept.)

Greece replied Nov. 22 and reportedly rejected the Turkish demands. The delivery of the reply was announced by Greek Foreign Min. Panayotis Pipinelis. Pipinelis denied that the Turkish note was an ultimatum. "Our main concern," he said, "is to ease tension." Turkish Foreign Min. Ishan Sabri Caglayangil also affirmed that Turkey had put no time limit on its demand for the removal of Greek troops from Cyprus.

Archbishop Makarios III, ethnarch of the Orthodox Church of Cyprus, leader of the Greek Cypriot community and president of Cyprus, said in a broadcast Nov. 24: Turkey "may force war on us. Whether the war which threatens... will be avoided or not does not depend on us."

A spokesman for the UN Emergency Force in Cyprus (UNFICYP), stationed on the island in 1964 when violence flared between Turkish and Greek Cypriots, said Nov. 15 that the UN had protested to the Nicosia regime against interferences with UN forces in the area. The note said the National Guard had disarmed UN troops, seized UN weapons and disabled UN radio equipment.

International Peace Moves

The U.S. appealed Nov. 16 to the Greek and Turkish Cypriot communities and to King Constantine for restraint. UN Secy. Gen. U Thant had discussed the crisis in separate meetings with the UN delegates from Greece, Turkey and Cyprus Nov. 15. U.S., UN and NATO representatives met with Greek, Turkish and Cypriot officials in their respective capitals Nov. 23-28. The envoys were: ex-U.S. Deputy Defense Secy. Cyrus R. Vance, appointed by Pres. Lyndon B. Johnson Nov. 22 as his special aide in the crisis; UN Undersecy. (for special political affairs) Jose Rolz-Bennett, representing UN Secy. Gen. Thant; NATO Secy. Gen. Manlio Brosio.

Vance met with Greek and Turkish leaders in Athens and Ankara Nov. 23-28. He was reported Nov. 27 to have proposed this formula to resolve the dispute: Greece and Turkey would remove from Cyprus those troops not authorized by the 1960 independence accord; Greece and Turkey would reaffirm their previous pledges to respect the independence and integrity of Cyprus; Turkey would demobilize the troops it had massed at the start of the crisis; the Cypriot police force would be reorganized by or under the supervision of the 4,500-man UNFICYP.

A plan proposed by Canadian Prime Min. Lester B. Pearson was presented to Greek Foreign Min. Pipinelis Nov. 22 by the U.S., British and Canadian ambassadors in Athens. The plan called for a reduction of Greek and Turkish troops in Cyprus, an expansion of UNFICYP's powers and the barring of Gen. Grivas from Cyprus. Pipinelis summoned the 3 ambassadors Nov. 23 and reportedly expressed partial approval of the Canadian proposal.

Brosio and Rolz-Bennett met with Greek officials in Athens Nov. 26, conferred with each other and then left for Ankara and Nicosia, respectively. Makarios was reported Nov. 27 to have told Rolz-Bennett that he favored (a) the withdrawal of Greek and Turkish troops from Cyprus with a view toward the island's eventual demilitarization, (b) the retention of UNFICYP troops.

The UN Security Council Nov. 25 unanimously approved a resolution calling on all sides in the Cyprus dispute to exercise restraint to avert war. UN Secy. Gen. Thant had issued similar pleas Nov. 22 and 24. The Council's resolution, adopted by consensus without a vote, requested that all interested parties "assist and cooperate in keeping peace and arriving at a permanent settlement." The Council had been called into emergency session Nov. 24 at the request of Zenon Rossides, chief delegate of Cyprus. Rossides urged the Council to adopt a resolution "to protect the territorial integrity, the sovereignty and political independence of Cyprus from...invasion by Turkey." Turkish delegate Orhan Eralp charged that the only threat to peace in Cyprus was "the presence of the illegal Greek army of occupation, which has been brought to the island surreptitiously and with the collusion of the Greek Cypriot administration." Dimitri Bitsios, chief Greek delegate, warned that "the unleashing of aggression" by Turkey "is imminent."

Thant Nov. 22 had expressed concern over the "military preparations, the movement of forces and threatening statements" in the Cyprus dispute. Thant's views were outlined in parallel messages to Makarios, Greek Premier Constantine V. Kollias and Turkish Premier Suleyman Demirel. Thant urged the 3 leaders "to avoid any action that could precipitate a new outbreak of hostilities and to exercise the utmost restraint in the present explosive circumstances." Thant informed them of his decision to send Rolz-Bennett to Cyprus, Greece and Turkey "to assist them in all possible ways to reduce the present tension."

In a 2d message to Makarios, Kollias and Demirel, Thant Nov. 24 stressed the need for the removal of Greek and Turkish troops from Cyprus. Thant said "tensions could be eased and the imminent threat of war removed by . . .[an] effort by the 3 parties directly concerned to . . . arrange for a substantial reduction [and eventual total withdrawal] of non-Cypriot forces now in hostile confrontation" on Cyprus. Thant suggested that the withdrawal could be carried out in phases and thus "make possible the positive demilitarization of Cyprus." He offered his "assistance in carrying out such a program and in continuing to help maintain quiet."

Greece & Turkey Agree to Reduce Troops

Representatives of Greece and Turkey Dec. 3, 1967 signed an agreement to reduce the number of the armed forces each had stationed in Cyprus.

The Greek ambassador in Ankara informed the Turkish foreign minister Jan. 17, 1968 that Greece had completed its troop withdrawal Jan. 16 — the final day of the 45-day time limit permitted under the Dec. 3 agreement. The number of

Greek troops withdrawn was estimated at 7,000-8,000, but no official figures were released. The removal of Turkish troops as called for under the Dec. 3 agreement was reported completed by mid-Jan. 1968.

UN Secy. Gen. Thant told the UN Security Council Mar. 9, 1968 that there had been "a significant lessening of tension" in the period ending Mar. 8. He proposed that Greece and Turkey assist UNFICYP "by encouraging the respective communities in Cyprus to display a spirit of conciliation and understanding."

Little in the way of strife was reported from Cyprus thereafter until 1970, when extensive damage was caused on the island by a series of bomb explosions beginning about Jan. 1. George Papadopoulos, who had become premier of Greece Dec. 13, 1967, met with Cypriot Pres. Makarios in Athens Jan. 17, 1970, and the 2 leaders denounced the extremism and violence that had taken place recently within the Greek community of Cyprus. The violence was attributed by authorities to a militant organization seeking an end to the independence of Cyprus in favor of *enosis,* or union with Greece.

ROYAL COUNTER-COUP FAILS

Constantine Fails to Unseat Junta

King Constantine attempted unsuccessfully Dec. 13, 1967 to overturn the junta. He appealed to his countrymen to join him in toppling the military rulers. The abortive counter-coup began after the king and his family flew to the city of Larissa in Thessaly early Dec. 13. From Larissa shortly before noon the king, on a rarely-listened-to short-wave radio station, broadcast an appeal to the Greek people to "close ranks" with him.

The forced withdrawal of Greek troops from Cyprus, agreed to by Turkey and Greece Dec. 3, 1967, had been viewed by many Greek army officers, according to observers, as a humiliating defeat for the junta. The king, observers reported, saw this as an opportunity to strike out against the military regime.

The king said that he had been forced to accept the junta's 1967 military coup "as an accomplished fact to avoid pointless bloodshed" but that he was "no longer willing to risk" the consolidation of the junta's power "under the threat of arms turned against my people and myself." The king charged that the junta was engaged in an "effort creating the establishment of a totalitarian regime." The king also declared that in opposing the military junta, he would not reach an "understanding with the Communists, who work out the nation's disaster."

In concluding his address from Larissa, the king said: "Today, I put an end to anomaly and to violence. I ask the Greek people as a whole to assist me in reestablishing in this

King Constantine II

country the moral values which were born in this land and from which all civilized peoples take their moral, social, economic and cultural development."

While the king was making his broadcast, supporters in several Greek air force planes dropped copies of his appeal over Salonika, the Macedonian city known for its liberal sentiment.

Shortly after noon, tanks and pro-government army units in Athens took up positions around the parliament building, the Defense Ministry, the royal palace and the radio station. Then a junta spokesman told the Greek people in a broadcast that "a criminal conspiracy and an attempt to abolish the state and lawful order" had taken place. The broadcast continued: "Common adventurers, motivated by foolish ambitions and ignoring the nation's interests, misled the king and led him astray and forced him as well to turn against the national revolution, against the calm and quiet of the people." 17 minutes later, the junta broadcast that "everything is under complete control."

Another junta broadcast announced Dec. 13 that Lt. Gen. George Zoitakis, 57, had been named as "viceroy" and "regent" of Greece with all the powers of King Constantine. Archbishop Ieronymos Kotsonis, who had been Constantine's private confessor and head of the Greek Church, gave the oath of office to the regent. A new cabinet was also sworn in Dec. 13 at General Staff headquarters in Athens; its members: *Premier and Defense Minister* — Col. George Papadopoulos; *Deputy Premier and Interior* — Brig. Gen. Stylianos Pattakos; *Economic Coordination* — Col. Nikolaos Makarezos; *Education* — Theofilaktos Papakonstantinou; *Commerce* — George Papadimitrakopoulos; *Agriculture* — Alexandros Matthaiou; *Labor* — Demetrios Pouleas; *Public Works* — Constantine Papadimitriou; *Industry* —

Constantine Kypraios; *Merchant Marine*—Vice Adm. Athanasios Athanasiou; *Social Welfare*—Efstathios Poulantzas.

At a Dec. 14 news conference, Papadopoulos, the new premier, said: The junta had first heard of the king's plan when Lt. Gen. Odysseus Anghelis, chief of the army general staff, received a letter from Constantine at 11:00 a.m. Dec. 13. The letter said the king was taking over control of the government and the armed forces. The junta met immediately but was unable to locate Premier Kollias. By its loss of contact with several army units, the junta was able to deduce that the king was in Larissa and then Kavalla. There were later reports "that the commander of the 3d Army Corps [Lt. Gen. George Peridis] and the leader of the armored division [Brig. Andreas Hoerschelmann] had attempted to refuse obedience to the legal government and had been placed in isolation." There were reports at 3:15 a.m. Dec. 14 that "2 Dakotas [aircraft] had taken off from Kavalla for an unknown destination." The junta later learned that the royal family and Kollias had arrived in Rome. Papadopoulos also said that an amnesty had been granted to the officers who appeard to have sided with the king during the coup attempt. But he added: "A very few of the protagonists may be subjected to administrative sanctions."

Among officers reported to have supported the king and, therefore, subject to "sanctions," were Peridis, Hoerschelmann, Brig. Orestes Vigalis, Peridis' chief of staff, and Adms. Dedas and Rozakis, naval commanders. Gen. Emanuel Kehagias and his deputy, Col. Mandakos, Kavalla military leaders, were reported arrested Dec. 14. Pericles Baklavas, owner and editor of *Prioni,* a Kavalla daily that had supported the king's proclamation, was arrested Dec. 15. Gen. Nikatas Zalahoris, a former division commander along the tense Turkish border, defected to Turkey Dec. 14 and sought political asylum.

King in Exile, Refuses Junta Terms to Return

King Constantine, who had failed to rally support from key military officers, flew to Rome early Dec. 14 with his family and close supporters, including Premier Constantine V. Kollias and Athens Mayor George Plytas. The king and his family spent Dec. 14 at the Greek embassy in Rome, and then went to the Rome villa of Prince Heinrich of Hesse, a distant cousin of the king's.

During the next few days Constantine met with representatives of the Greek military junta to discuss terms under which the king might return to Greece. They found, however, that their disagreement was too deep for an early reconciliation. The king also met Dec. 15-16 with Foreign Min. Panayotis Pipinelis (who was reconfirmed as foreign minister three days later) and Dec. 16 with Archbishop Ieronymos Kotsonis.

Pro-royalist Greek sources indicated that the delegation had set forth demands that would have made the king a virtual puppet of the junta. The king, in turn, was said to have insisted on the following points for his return: (1) There must be a return to normal political life, with free elections, at a specified date, open to all parties except the Communists. (2) There must be no reprisals against anyone who supported the king in his counter-coup attempt. (3) No restrictions should be placed on the king's family or selection of staff. (4) Papadopoulos must be replaced as premier by a civilian.

Brig. Stylianos Pattakos, the deputy premier, said in Athens Dec. 16 that the king had not forfeited his right to the throne but that in order for him to return to Greece "certain procedures will have to be observed because in cases such as this certain dislikes build up." Meanwhile, Pattakos also announced that Athens Mayor George Plytas had been dismissed and that the defense minister, Gen. George Spandidakis, had been relieved of his post Dec. 13 after he refused to return from NATO headquarters to lead the armed forces against the king.

Constantine, who had been living in the Greek embassy in Rome since going into exile, moved Feb. 16, 1968 to the Eden Hotel. The *N.Y. Times* reported Feb. 18 that the Greek government had told the king he was no longer welcome in the embassy.

Premier Papadopoulos announced Dec. 22 that a new constitution would be submitted to the Greek people early in 1968 but that free elections would be delayed until "the aims of the revolution of Apr. 21 had been realized and the risks of communism excluded." The following day he announced that a plebiscite on the constitution would be held Apr. 21, 1968, if "humanly possible." If the referendum were not held by this date, he said, it would be held no later than Sept. 15, 1968.

3 of the principal junta members — Col. Papadopoulos, the premier, Brig. Pattakos, the deputy premier, and Col. Makarezos, economic coordination minister — relinquished their commissions in the army Dec. 20, 1967 and became civilians.

International Ramifications

U.S. State Department officials held Dec. 14, 1967 that the Greek military junta had lost its claim to legitimacy after King Constantine had been forced into exile. But they denied reports that the U.S. was withholding formal recognition of the new regime. State Secy. Dean Rusk said that the U.S. would "wait for awhile" before reaching a decision on recognizing the military government. He said that the U.S. hoped "that Greece will move as promptly as possible toward constitutional government." (The U.S. resumed diplomatic relations with Greece Jan. 23, 1968.)

British Prime Min. Harold Wilson said Dec. 14 that with the exile of King Constantine, the "whole question of British recognition of the Greek regime does come up for consideration." (Britain, however, resumed relations with Greece Jan. 25, 1968.) Answering questions in the House of Commons, Wilson assailed "the barbarous methods in use in Greece."

The ambassadors of Italy, Britain, France, West Germany and the U.S. in Athens ignored an invitation to meet with Premier George Papadopoulos Dec. 14.

The Greek Foreign Ministry recalled the Greek ambassador to Sweden Feb. 29, 1968 and protested to the Swedish and Danish embassies in Athens about their hostile attitudes towards the junta. The junta accused Denmark of "blunt intervention in Greece's domestic affairs."

The 18-nation Council of Europe had voted Jan. 31 to expel or suspend Greece from membership if parliamentary democracy were not restored by the spring of 1969. The council's representative for Greek affairs, Dr. Max van der Stoel, of the Netherlands, said he doubted the junta would meet the spring deadline. In May the Consultative Assembly of the Council of Europe met and heard a report by van der Stoel, who had made a fact-finding visit to Greece Apr. 22-28. He provided this summary of his main conclusions: (1) The Greek regime was "still a dictatorship in which the state of siege is continued, the majority of human rights and fundamental freedoms suspended, and considerable restrictions imposed by the government." (2) The press was still censored; political discussion or the functioning of political parties was impossible. (3) The organization of any political opposition was prevented. (4) A draft constitution prepared by the Constitutional Commission was less liberal than the 1952 constitution; it imposed greater restrictions on human rights and fundamental freedoms. (5) Despite "formal promises" from several members of the regime to restore parliamentary democracy, no "definite assurances" had been given as to time limits and conditions for this. "Contradictory answers" had been given as to when the state of siege would be lifted and as to whether the constitution would take effect fully and immediately after the referendum. (6) It was important that the "democratic forces" in Greece should agree on a "joint program" and that Greece's friends and allies, especially the U.S., should "exert all their influence to enable her to return to democracy within the coming year."

GREECE UNDER THE JUNTA

Amnesty, Prisoners & Arrests

After 8 months during which the junta consolidated its control over Greece, Premier George Papadopoulos Dec. 23, 1967 announced a Christmas amnesty for certain persons arrested since the coup. Papadopoulos said that the amnesty would include persons involved in the *Aspida* (Shield) secret army group, which was alleged to have plotted to overthrow the monarchy and to install a left-wing regime. The amnesty, Papadopoulos added, would not include "the Communists who have been condemned for criminal acts before the revolution and the terrorists who have been arrested since the revolution."

Andreas Papandreou, son of ex-Premier George Papandreou, was released from prison under the amnesty Dec. 24. Ex-Premiers George Papandreou and Panayotis Kanellopoulos were released from house detention Dec. 23, and 7 army officers who had been convicted of *Aspida* activities were released from prison Dec. 25. (Government spokesmen had said in Athens May 4 that Andreas Papandreou would stand trial within 5 days on charges of treason for his involvement in the alleged *Aspida* conspiracy. The government May 6 published a letter allegedly sent by the elder Papandreou to Col. Alexandros Papaterpos, then director of intelligence. The letter, denounced by George Papandreou May 8 as a forgery, said that Papandreou would "give anything that is necessary for the *Aspida* [group]." Commenting on the letter, government spokesmen said: "The lies, the official lies, which George Papandreou told from the rostrum of Parliament, which he had turned into a suburban coffee house, and which consisted in refusal, insults, violence and threats, have now been revealed." "The letter, in monstrous clarity, shivering in cynicism, categorically gives a clear answer to all those who still have the naivete to believe the shameless lies of Papandreou.")*

Public Order Ministry Secy. Gen. Ioannis Ladas said Dec. 24 that only about 300 persons would be included in the amnesty. Ladas announced Dec. 26 that the more than 2,500 prisoners being held on the islands of Leros and Yioura would not benefit from the amnesty. At least 80 political prisoners were reported freed by Dec. 26; 86 were released from Leros and Yioura Jan. 29, 1968; 80 more were freed Mar. 2, and 100 were released Apr. 18. Mrs. Vasso Katrakis, the painter and engraver, was among those released from Yioura.

Mrs. Helen Vlachos (Vlachou), a conservative Greek publisher who had been kept under house arrest, told reporters in London Dec. 22, 1967 that she had dyed her hair and slipped past guards around her Athens apartment Dec. 15 and fled to England. Mrs. Vlachos said that she had arrived in London Dec. 18-19 and had gone to the offices of the British Broadcasting Corp. to seek help. The British Home Office Dec. 22 gave Mrs. Vlachos permission to remain in Britain as a visitor indefinitely. Mrs. Vlachos had been arrested Sept. 28 for criticizing the junta. She had ceased publication of her 2 Athens dailies, *Kathimerini* and *Messimvrini,* and her weekly magazine, *Eikones,* after the Apr. 21 coup. Mrs. Vlachos had said at a press conference Sept. 24 that the junta had failed to keep its promise to restore freedom of the press. She pledged to keep her papers shut down as long as censorship continued.

(The government announced May 12, 1968 that censorship of all Greek magazines was ended, but the press remained under strict government control.)

---

* The government confirmed May 23, 1967 that the body of Nikiforos Mandelaras, 39, had been found washed up on the island of Rhodes May 21. Mandelaras had been a defense counsel in the *Aspida* trial and was to have been a Center Union candidate in elections cancelled by the junta.

Ioannis Kapsis, editor of the Athens daily *Ethnos (Nation),* was arrested by security police in Athens Jan. 18, 1968, and Christos Lambrakis, owner of 5 Athens publications, was also arrested. Both, reported to have been personal friends of Andreas Papandreou, had previously been under arrest but had been released in the 1967 Christmas amnesty.

A military tribunal on Crete convicted 16 persons of anti-government activities Feb. 2. 19 co-defendants were acquitted. Those convicted included Fibos Ioannides, ex-secretary of the Center Union's youth organization on Crete, who received a 110-year prison sentence. Pericles Ghika, a former member of the Greek intelligence service, was sentenced to life imprisonment Mar. 20 for allegedly selling military and diplomatic information to Albanian and Italian authorities during 1960-6.

Demetrios Papaspyrou, president of Greece's last parliament, was put under house arrest Apr. 17 after he gave foreign newspapers statements criticizing the junta. Ex-Center Union Deputies Anghelos Anghelousis and Efstathios Anthopoulos were arrested Apr. 16 and 17 for deportation to the prison islands.

3 ousted army officers, including Brig. Andreas Hoerschelmann, were arrested in Athens Feb. 24.

Ex-Economic Coordination Min. George Mavros (of Center Union) and ex-Interior Min. George Rallis (of ERE) were placed under house arrest May 1. Rallis had defied martial law Apr. 30 by issuing a statement to foreign correspondents in which he called for the return of the king and for free elections. In his statement, Rallis accused the military government of intending "to hang onto power disregarding the danger that the Communists might take this opportunity to turn Greece into a European Vietnam."

Dr. Ikovos Diamantopoulos, a former vice president of parliament, was also placed under house arrest.

Ex-Premier Constantine Kollias, who had supported King Constantine during his attempt to overthrow the military junta, was arrested July 13.

3 persons were sentenced to prison July 8 for plotting to overthrow the military regime, but 18 defendants tried with them were set free. Those jailed were naval petty officers charged with planting 2 bombs in downtown Athens. They were supposedly part of the Democratic Defense underground resistance group.

Press Secy. Michael Sideratos had reported Apr. 8, 1968 that after the 1967 military coup 6,848 persons had been arrested; since then 3,803 regarded as not dangerous had been released, and 608 had been set free because of age or health or because they were women. Sideratos added that the 2,437 still detained were "highly dangerous Communists, and it is certain that if they were set free, most of them would turn into armed terrorists."

Andreas Papandreou Leaves Greece, Forms Liberation Group

Andreas Papandreou, a former naturalized U.S. citizen who had served in the Center Union government of his father, ex-Premier George Papandreou, left Greece Jan. 16, 1968 and flew to Paris. Papandreou, held as a political prisoner since the military coup but freed in the December amnesty, had been indicted by the junta on charges of high treason in connection with his alleged leadership of the *Aspida* conspiracy. While in prison, Papandreou, who had been an economics professor in the U.S., had been offered teaching positions by 3 U.S. universities — UCLA, Brandeis and Northwestern. U.S. State Department sources said Jan. 9 that Papandreou would be granted a U.S. visa if he requested one.

In his first public statement since his release, Papandreou said in Paris Jan. 18 that the junta was the most "oppressive and dictatorial" regime in Greece's history. He said the democratic countries had a "moral responsibility" to help remove the junta because "the junta... derives its power... from the weapons given to it by its allies."

Papandreou said Jan. 20 that he thought King Constantine should remain in exile until democratic rule was restored in Greece. Papandreou added that if the king returned sooner, "all the onus of the regime will be transferred to him." Papandreou credited his release from prison to the pressure put on the junta by foreign intellectuals, "especially the American university community."

In February Papandreou formed an underground organization, the Pan-Hellenic Liberation Movement (PAK). In a statement issued in March, Papandreou said: "PAK is a liberation movement. It is intended to provide the focus for coordination both at home and abroad of the liberation efforts of the Greek people.... Its platform is restricted to one single objective: to establish in Greece the sovereignty of the Greek people — so the Greek people may choose freely among competing parties and party platforms in the context of a genuinely democratic process."

In a speech before the Americans for Democratic Action in Washington Mar. 9, Papandreou condemned the U.S. for recognizing the Greek junta and the NATO alliance for continuing to arm the junta. He declared that "the Greek people have no alternative but to organize their own resistance." He accused the junta of using "physical violence that transcends Nazi techniques" on political prisoners. He added that "if the junta were isolated morally, militarily and economically, it would collapse of its own weight."

Papandreou attended an international reflective summit conference of nearly 100 intellectuals that was held at Princeton University Dec. 1-15, 1968 to discuss, and at times debate, "The United States, Its Problems, Its Image and Its Impact on the World." In an address at the seminar, Papandreou asserted that torture in Greek concentration camps "surpasses the tortures which have been perpetrated at Dachau." He charged that the U.S. Central Intelligence Agency had aided the Greek military junta in its takeover of Apr. 1967. Greece "has become a fascist beachhead," he declared. "Once this thing begins it has a tendency to spread. It is like a cancer." Papandreou expressed his gratitude to

"Arthur Schlesinger and those who joined him in preparing a resolution for the total cessation of military, economic and moral aid to the military regime in Athens on the part of both the U.S.A. and its NATO allies."

George Papandreou Condemns Junta

Ex-Premier George Papandreou, who had been released from house arrest Dec. 23, 1967, was again placed under house detention Apr. 15, 1968, as was ex-Premier Panayotis Kanellopoulos. A junta spokesman said they were arrested for "excessive political activity that might endanger public security and order."

In a statement smuggled out of Greece Apr. 17, Papandreou charged that the junta had abolished freedoms of the press, speech and assembly in Greece. He appealed to the free world to join in a boycott aimed at toppling the military regime. Papandreou noted that the military had taken power by claiming that there was an impending Communist takeover. Papandreou said that the junta had been investigating since it came to power "and has failed to discover even a single weapon, either among the democratic camp or even among the Communists." "The truth is," he charged, "that the myth of the Communist danger was manufactured and the coup undertaken only to prevent our [the Center Union's] electoral victory." Papandreou asserted that although the junta said it was ending corruption, "never before, not even during the worst period of parliamentarianism, has there been such demagogy and such favoritism. All those who have been voted into office have been dismissed without exception... and have been replaced by relatives and favorites." He charged that to "utter a word of criticism" of the junta was forbidden under pain of "long-term imprisonment.... In fact, even without uttering a word, thousands of citizens are arrested and deported to desolate islands...."

Ioannis Apostolides, director general of the Press Ministry, said Apr. 18 that the government would take no further action against George Papandreou. Apostolides said the ex-premier ·had asked the world "to isolate his own country" because he was "trying to get back into power."

Torture of Prisoners Charged

James Becket, a Massachusetts attorney, and Anthony Marreco, a British lawyer, charged Jan. 27, 1968 that Greek police had practiced widespread, sadistic torture of political prisoners. The 2 men, acting as representatives of Amnesty International (London), filed their report, entitled "Situation in Greece," after a one-month investigation in Athens. Amnesty International (London) Apr. 6 published a 2d report entitled "Torture of Political Prisoners in Greece." Anthony Marreco, who filed this report, told of 14 prisoners tortured by the Greek police.

Greek Press Secy. Michael Sideratos Apr. 8 rejected Amnesty International's charges as untrue. He said that while in Greece, Marreco had insisted on speaking with prisoners convicted or awaiting trial for sabotage attempts. Sideratos admitted that there could have been individual cases of police brutality. Sideratos presented a report by the International Committee of the Red Cross (IRC) that indicated no complaints of rough treatment by interviewed prisoners. The report had been compiled between Jan. 29 and Feb. 21 by 2 IRC representatives who had visited the prison islands of Leros and Yioura. The report, however, did recommend improvements to alleviate overcrowding and inadequate heating.

A defector from the Greek navy's South Aegean Command, Lt. (j.g.) Constantine Marotis-Lanas, said in New York Mar. 20 that he had received many reports of executions while serving with the security police in the port of Piraeus. Marotis-Lanas charged that the Piraeus security police had a torture chamber, and he described at least one case of torture. Marotis-Lanas was presented at a press conference by Andreas Papandreou.

In a London *Times* report published Feb. 25, 1968, Miss Tonia Marketaki, a Greek journalist and film producer, had related that while being held prisoner by the police in Athens, she saw one man who was put "into a solitary cell next to our room. When we went to the toilet we could look through the hole in his door. He spoke a little but he seemed almost dead. His legs, feet and head appeared to have been beaten. He could not lie down because he could not bear to put his head on the floor. He was on his knees most of the time. I believe he was a victim of the *falanga* torture: a prisoner is tied to a bench and beaten from the feet up."

The London *Times* Apr. 11 printed excerpts from several signed statements, allegedly smuggled out of the Partheni prison camp on Leros Island, that told of conditions of "inhuman isolation and moral torture."

One of 21 defendants charged with sedition before an Athens court-martial revoked his confession July 3 on the ground that it had been made under torture. Gerassimos Notaras, a noted political sociologist, claimed that he had been beaten on the soles of his feet, subjected to electrical shock, and threatened with being thrown into the sea if he did not confess.

In the latter part of Nov. 1968 4 former political prisoners were sent to Strasbourg by the Greek government to testify before the European Human Rights Commission that they had not been tortured. 2 of the 4 promptly escaped and testified instead that security police had tortured them "beyond anyone's imagination" to extract confessions of anti-junta activity. They said they had been given electric shocks, had been clubbed on the soles of their feet and had been beaten with sandbags. At a press conference called in Strasbourg a junta spokesman stated that the 2 men had not defected but had been "kidnapped by terrorists" from the Pan-Hellenic Liberation Organization (PAK).

Several persons accused of belonging to the underground resistance organization Democratic Defense were placed on trial before the Salonika court-martial Nov. 6. According to testimony submitted to the Council of Europe, the prisoners had been tortured in an attempt to obtain confessions from them and induce them to give testimony against others. Among the defendants were: Stelios Nestor, a lawyer and member of the Council of World University Service, and Pavlos Zannas, a member of the International Federation of Movie Critics.

Junta Ousts Dissidents

The government Jan. 3, 1968 dismissed 4 of Greece's highest banking officials. Those ousted were: Prof. Ioannis Paraskevopoulos, governor of the Bank of Greece since 1964 and premier in 2 caretaker governments; Constantine Eliascos and Spilios Kapadais, National Bank deputy governors; and Spyros Loverdos, governor of the Hellenic Industrial Development Bank. No reason for the dismissals was given.

The Holy Synod, executive body of the Greek Orthodox Church, announced Jan. 16 the arraignment of 2 church prelates — Archbishop Iakovos, primate of Greece for 2 weeks during 1962, and Bishop Panteleimon, metropolitan of Salonika since 1951. They were to face a church tribunal on charges of "behavior unbecoming to a cleric." Panteleimon was reported to have refused to officiate at ceremonies attended by junta members.

It was reported that as of Feb. 5, 1968, some 101 army officers, including 37 generals, and 19 air force officers, including 5 generals, had been dismissed for their support of King Constantine in his attempted abortive counter-coup.

During the week ended Mar. 2, 967 government employes were dismissed, ostensibly for backing the king. Ex-Premier Constantine Kollias, who had gone into exile with the king but who later returned to Greece to resume the practice of law, was dismissed as Supreme Court chief prosecutor at the end of January. 56 university professors and assistant professors were charged with disloyalty and dismissed Jan. 27, and 4 senior ambassadors were dismissed Feb. 1.

The government May 29 dismissed 30 judges, most of them for allegedly being Center Union followers. The judges were ousted during a 3-day suspension of their life tenure. They included 7 Supreme Court judges and prosecutors and Stylianos Mavromihalis, Supreme Court president since 1963 and a caretaker premier in 1963. Theodoros Kamberis, Supreme Court vice president, was named May 31 to replace Mavromihalis. Justice Min. Constantine Kalambokias was appointed vice president of the court and was to keep his cabinet post. Constantine Thanopoulos, a Supreme Court justice, was named chief prosecutor, replacing Constantine Kollias.

Government Posts Redistributed

Premier Papadopoulos carried out a major shift of his cabinet June 20, 1968. He dropped 9 civilian ministers and replaced them with 10 civilian ministers and undersecretaries. The new cabinet members were sworn in the same day. The principal change involved the replacement of 2d Deputy Premier Nikolaos Makarezos with Dimitrios Patilis, a retired general; Makarezos, 3d in line in the junta's dominant inner triumvirate, retained his position as economic coordination minister. (Patilis was believed to have joined the inner power group. This promotion was considered a reward for his role in helping to block the king's counter-coup.)

Papadopoulos said the cabinet change had been carried out "to improve the condition of the government's functioning, leading to a more rapid and effective accomplishment of the aims of the revolution." The new cabinet: Ministers— *Premier and Defense*— Papadopoulos; *First Deputy Premier and Interior*—Stylianos Pattakos; *2d Deputy Premier*—

Patilis; *Economic Coordination*—Makarezos; *Foreign*—
Panayotis Pipinelis; *Joint Minister of Coordination*—
Ioannis Rodinos-Orlandos; *Justice*—Prof. Ioannis
Triandafylopoulos; *Education & Religion*—Theofylaktos
Papaconstantinou; *Finance*—Adamantios Androutsopoulos;
Trade—Epamiondas Tsellos; *Industry*—Constantine
Kypraios; *Public Works*—Constantine Papadimitriou;
Communications—Spyridon Lizardos; *Agriculture*—
Alexandros Matthaiou; *Social Welfare*—Prof. Loukas
Patras; *Merchant Marine*—Prof. Ioannis Holevas; *Labor*—
Apostolos Voyazis; *Public Order*—Panayotis Tzevelekos.
Undersecretaries—*Economic Coordination*—Ioulios
Evlamrlambios; *Finance*—Nikitas Sioris; *Premier's
Office*—Constantine Vololinis; *Welfare*—Elias Dimitras;
Agriculture—George Tsistopoulos; *Permanent
Undersecretary for Foreign Affairs*—George
Christopoulos.

Papadopoulos shifted 4 members of the ruling Revolutionary Council Nov. 21 for the purpose of "exploiting the
talents of these people where they are best suited." 2 of the
council members balked at their reassignments and resigned
Nov. 25. Ex.-Col. Demetrios Stamatelopoulos, secretary
general for communications, was ordered to exchange his
post with ex-Col. Michael Balopoulos, secretary general for
tourism. Ex-Col. Ioannis Ladas, secretary general of the
Public Order Ministry (security chief), and ex-Col. Petros
Kotsellis, secretary general of the Interior Ministry, also
exchanged posts. The 2 Council members who quit Nov. 25
in protest against their reappointments were
Stamatelopoulos and Balopoulos. Ladas and Kotsellis
accepted reassignment. (It had been rumored in Athens in
early 1968 that Ladas had been suspected of plotting his own
counter-coup within the junta. Ladas was understood to be
more conservative than the rest of the junta members.)

(Education & Religious Affairs Min. Theophylaktos
Papaconstantinou resigned June 9, 1969 because of what he
described as his inability to "serve conscientiously" under the
circumstances.)

Economic Developments

The *Economist Foreign Report* asserted Mar. 14, 1968 that "after almost a year in office, the Greek military regime is probably affecting the ordinary man more economically than politically.... Several textile factories are working only one shift, instead of the 3 which were normal before the April coup. According to one estimate, about 20% of the textile workers have had to be discharged.... Particularly hard hit have been the stores dealing in electrical goods. One major store, in the heart of Athens, has had to close down because of lack of demand.... The regime skillfully contrives to conceal these depressing facts from the public. The index of industrial production [however] showed a 20% drop for 1967 as compared with 1966."

Stavros Niarchos and Aristotle Onassis announced May 5 and 7 that they had decided to transfer their foreign-flag shipping companies — Niarchos (London), Ltd. and Springfield Shipping Co. of Panama — to Greece. The Greek government had urged Greek shipowners to transfer their foreign-registered shipping fleets to Greek registry, and it had offered major tax concessions. Several other Greek shipowners announced similar decisions later.

The cancellation of all debts to the Agricultural Bank was announced in April. The amount involved was officially estimated at $270 million.

The U.S. Department of Commerce weekly *International Commerce* reported May 6 that the Chase Manhattan Bank and the Bank of America "are planning shortly to establish branch offices in Greece." In addition, "through tax and other incentives, the [Greek] government has so far enticed 25 firms, 8 of which are American, to establish regional supervisory offices in Greece." But the weekly said the Greek balance of payments had worsened during 1967 because of "decreases in tourist earnings, emigrant remittances and capital inflows."

In a speech delivered June 1, Coordination Min. Makarezos announced that the Greek economy had been on the verge of collapse at the time of the coup in 1967 but that the junta had changed a prospective balance-of-payments deficit into a gain of $13.5 million in foreign exchange.

Junta Wins Approval of Charter

The military junta July 11, 1968 made public a 138-article draft constitution designed to return civilian rule to the country. A slightly revised version of the constitution was approved by Greece's voters Sept. 29 and was put into effect Nov. 15. In presenting the draft July 11, Premier George Papadopolous said it would be put to a national referendum Sept. 29. No timetable was given for parliamentary elections or for the return of exiled King Constantine. The new charter would strip the king of many of his powers, separate the executive and legislative branches of government, increase the independence of the armed forces and increase the authority of the executive.

Among major provisions of the draft constitution:

●The king was proclaimed the "symbol of the nation's unity." Constantine was to return to Greece at the time of the first parliamentary election, although "the government may invite the king to return at an earlier date." The king would be titular head of the armed forces but no longer would be their commander-in-chief. He could appoint or dismiss the premier only with the approval of parliament or the new Council of the Nation. (A provision considered humiliating to the king and queen charged the government with responsibility for assuring "that the crown prince should receive an education compatible with the high office to which he is destined.") The king could refuse to ratify some legislation, but he would be forced to ratify bills reintroduced in parliament after a waiting period of one month and reapproved by an absolute majority.

●A newly created Council of the Nation would be required to approve all changes in government, if parliament were unable to do so, and would be consulted by the king before parliament could be dissolved and new elections called. The council would consist of the premier, the speaker of parliament, leaders of parliamentary parties, the supreme court president, the president of the new 11-member Constitutional Court, the president of the Council of State (consisting of former premiers), chiefs of the armed forces and deans of the country's 3 principal universities.

●The new Constitutional Court, appointed by the government, was empowered to strip any person guilty of "struggling against the regime of crowned democracy" of his constitutional rights. The court could also ban parties "whose aims or activities are openly or covertly opposed to the fundamental principles of the regime, or aim at overthrowing the prevailing social order or expose to danger the territorial integrity of the state or its public security."

●Parliament would be reduced from 300 to not more than 150 members, about 1/6 of them appointed by the parties in proportion to their electoral strength. No member of parliament except the premier and the 2 deputy premiers could simultaneously be a government minister. "No one may be elected deputy for 4 consecutive parliamentary terms," except the premier or "leaders of parties recognized under the constitution and the rules of parliament." (Papadopoulos said that constitutional experts would have to decide whether or not this clause was to be retroactive in effect. If it were, about 98 members of Greece's last parliament would be disqualified from running.) Any person "who acquired the citizenship of a foreign country, even if he subsequently renounced it," was barred from serving in parliament. (It was understood that this provision was directed specifically at opposition leader Andreas Papandreou, who had renounced U.S. citizenship to become active in Greek politics.)

●The premier would be chosen from the party with a majority in parliament. If no party obtained a majority, parliament would choose a premier. (Papadopoulos said that he would announce the first parliamentary elections 45 days before they were held.)

●The role of the armed forces was defined as "the defense of national independence and territorial integrity of the nation, as well as of the prevailing regime and social order, from external or internal enemies." "The military owe faith and allegiance to the country, the national ideals and national traditions, and serve the nation." (No mention was made of the armed forces' former oath of allegiance to the king.) Officers' promotions would be decided by the armed forces and would be binding on the defense minister.

●Parliamentary motions of censure against the premier would be limited to annual intervals. The press would be forbidden to criticise the church or the king, to undermine the armed forces, to assist in overthrowing the state and to propagate illegal views or promote outlawed organizations.

●The martial law imposed in Apr. 1967 at the time of the military coup would remain in effect until lifted by parliament.

A copy of the draft constitution was given to King Constantine in Rome before it was made public, and his subsequent public silence on the matter was thought to indicate his assent to it.

Justice Min. Ioannis Triandafylopoulos resigned from the cabinet on July 8, reportedly because of a disagreement with other ministers over the draft constitution. The resignation of Education Undersecy. Dimitrios Koutsoyanopoulos was announced the same day. Both men had joined the cabinet June 20.

A revised draft of the charter was made public Sept. 16 by Premier Papadopoulos. The last article was changed to enable the junta to hold up the operation of 12 articles dealing with personal freedoms until the regime completed the "aims of the revolution." Among these articles were those dealing with the holding of free elections, freedom of the press, the right of assembly and association, the right to form trade unions and political parties and the right to protection from arbitrary house search, arrest and imprisonment.

The Greek electorate Sept. 29 gave an overwhelming vote of approval to the constitution submitted by the junta. The voting was held under military law, and an Aug. 6th decree had made balloting compulsory for all Greeks between the ages of 21 and 70 who lived within 300 miles of their voting district. The government viewed the election victory as a vote of approval for its military rule, but other observers held that Greeks saw the constitution as the possible first step on the road back to parliamentary democracy. According to the final referendum figures, 4,638,543 (or 91.87%) of the 5,048,981 votes cast were in favor of the constitution. 7.76% of the electorate (391,923 voters) voted "no," and 22.5% of the 6,516,285 registered voters did not cast ballots. 18,515 votes (.37%) were invalidated. The "no" votes in the Athens-Piraeus area totaled 22.7%, compared with 3.6% in the countryside. (A junta spokesman claimed Sept. 30 that the percentage of voters who abstained was "normal." Officials said that persons who did not have legitimate excuses for not voting would be prosecuted.)

Although the regime had claimed that the referendum would be a "free" election, all campaign posters seen before the election were reported to have urged a "yes" vote. Several politicians, however, had urged that the constitution be rejected. Responding to the government's call for open debate on the constitution, 3 former Center Union deputies — John Zigdis, Andreas Kokkevis and Gerasimos Vasilatos — said July 17 that the charter would nullify "the principle of the sovereignty of the people" and would "inevitably lead to a new period of trial for the country." Ex-Foreign Min. Evangelos Averoff, in an Aug. 18 newspaper article, urged the rejection of the constitution on the ground that it would "perpetuate the revolution and, in practice, establish the present regime as a permanent form of government in Greece." From the headquarters of the Pan-Hellenic Liberation Movement in Stockholm, Andreas Papandreou called on "the Greek people to vote 'no' to this monstrously totalitarian constitution, 'no' to the vulgar dictatorship." Constantine Mitsotakis, economic coordination minister under the government of George Papandreou, denounced the draft constitution in late July as a "fraud to deceive international public opinion." He said the only way to avert disaster would be to have the junta step down. Mitsotakis was reported Aug. 2 to have gone into hiding to avoid arrest.

7 former government officials, including ex-Premiers George Papandreou and Panayotis Kanellopoulos, had been released from house detention in a Sept. 23 amnesty. The 7 made no comment on the proposed constitution. Although Papadopoulos had announced Sept. 16 that he would free "all former politicians who did not commit crimes," 13 non-Communist former cabinet ministers were still held after the Sept. 23 amnesty. Papandreou and Kanellopoulos boycotted the constitutional referendum, but no action was taken against them. The other 5 released Sept. 23 were ex-Economic Coordination Min. George Mavros; ex-Interior Min. George Rallis; ex-Public Works Min. Stellos Allamanis; Demetrius Papaspyrou, last president of the Greek parliament; his deputy, Iakovos Diamantopoulos.

(The Greek government formally apologized Sept. 27 for intruding into the U.S. embassy in pursuit of a U.S. citizen who had displayed a poster urging Greeks to reject the junta-proposed constitution. Thea Tannenbaum, 19, daughter of Prof. Louis Tannenbaum of Colorado University, had put the *"Oxi"* [no] poster on the family car Sept. 26 in reaction to the vast government campaign urging Greek voters to approve the charter. After Greek police had picked up the family for questioning, the family managed to elude them momentarily, and Mrs. Tannenbaum ran into the U.S. embassy in Athens. A policeman followed her into the building and was attempting to drag her out when he was stopped by an embassy guard. After a full explanation was given, the Tannenbaums were permitted to leave Greece.)

Premier Papadopoulos announced Sept. 30 that the vote for the constitution had given "absolute national approval" to his government and had indicated the people's desire that "the work of the revolution must be fulfilled." He said his regime had been "democratically installed as of yesterday," and he pledged that the suspension of individual rights would be "only temporary, and democracy will be expanded with each passing day to the degree that its existence will be safeguarded."

The new constitution, which went into effect Nov. 15, replaced the 1952 constitution. The government had announced Nov. 6 that 2 of the charter's 12 suspended articles dealing with individual rights — those relating to freedom of assembly and association — would be in force when the charter became effective. But the Nov. 15 announcement said that the 2 provisions would be held in abeyance for technical reasons: the government decree reactivating the 2 provisions could not be published until the constitution became law. The government statement said that the 2 provisions applied only to trade unions' rights to free association and assembly.

Constitutional provisions granting wider power to the military and giving it a major role in safeguarding "the established political system and social order" went into effect Dec. 14. Under the new system, the cabinet's jurisdiction in military affairs was taken over by a newly established unified and largely autonomous military command. The command was to be headed by Lt. Gen. Odysseus Anghelis, chief of the defense and army general staffs, as chief of the armed forces, a new post. Anghelis was to be virtual defense minister with complete authority over the army, navy and air force. Military appointments, transfers, promotions and dismissals of officers, previously handled by the cabinet, would be carried out by service councils composed of generals. Defense policies would be drawn up by a Supreme Council of National Defense, represented by the premier, the deputy premier, the ministers of defense, economic coordination, interior and foreign affairs and the chief of the armed forces.

The government's chief spokesman, Vyron Stamatopoulos, confirmed Dec. 11 that the Revolutionary Council, which had ruled Greece since the 1967 coup, had been stripped of its powers under the new constitution, which had implied but did not specify this change. Stamatopoulos explained that "the regime's instruments of power are clearly defined in the new constitution. They are: the king, or the regent, the premier and the cabinet, and — at some later stage — parliament. No one else."

International Statements Condemn Junta

British Prime Min. Harold Wilson, addressing the House of Commons, condemned the Greek regime for committing what he described as "bestialities." London and Paris observers of Greek developments reported in July 1968 that Wilson's statements had been prompted by fears that the proposed new Greek constitution will strip the Greek king of all his effective powers. Great Britain had viewed the monarchy in Greece as an important source of stability in a country that had seen much political turmoil in recent years.

The International Commission of Jurists noted Aug. 14, in a statement entitled "The New Constitution of the Greek Colonels," that "no real discussion can take place under the shadow of martial law and police activities against non-conformists." The commission, a non-governmental organization holding consultative status with the UN Economic & Social Council and the Council of Europe, said: "It would be unwise to make a value judgement on the draft constitution itself.... With or without a constitution, a dictatorship is a dictatorship, and the most convincing safeguards are illusory. There is every indication that the colonels' draft is tailor-made to suit themselves.... It would not seem to be in the people's interest to approve a constitution which is no more than a legal instrument devised to keep the government in power. If the Greeks are to regain some part of their former freedom, those in authority must unequivocally retire from politics."

The Consultative Assembly of the Council of Europe Sept. 23 received from Dr. Max van der Stoel, the Council's representative for Greek affairs, a report based on conversations with the Greek government's official spokesmen, former ministers and deputies from various political parties, members of the diplomatic corps accredited to Athens, university professors and Greek and foreign journalists. He said in the report that: (a) there had been no "alleviation" of the dictatorship; (b) the draft constitution did not comply with democratic principles; (c) the referendum, to be held under the state of siege, had not been organized under "conditions of propriety, enabling everyone to conduct a free and democratic campaign"; (d) a majority supporting the constitution could not be considered as a vote of confidence in the current Greek regime. The only alternative to a perpetuation of the regime was its replacement by a "really representative government of national unity in which all democratic forces of the country would take part, and the main task of which would be the organization of free elections, the drafting of a really democratic constitution, and the return of the country to a normal situation and a democratic regime. I am convinced that such a government of national unity can be realized and that today its chances are better than ever before. It would seem to be the only way of preventing serious tensions in Greece. ... Now that it has become clear that there is a serious and constructive alternative ..., the time is ripe for a concerted effort by Greece's friends and allies to help to secure the establishment of such a government of national unity."

The Consultative Assembly Sept. 26 adopted a resolution calling for (a) the "immediate abolition of martial law" in Greece and (b) parliamentary elections, to be held within 6 months, in which every candidate would be allowed to conduct a free and democratic campaign. The resolution said that the assembly will follow events in Greece closely and would consider at its Jan. 1969 session whether or not to recommend the suspension of Greece from its right of representation in the Council of Europe.

Paul O'Dwyer, then the Democratic candidate for the U.S. Senate from New York State, called in July for an end to American "material and moral support to the Greek military regime." He said he thought "all aid to Greece" should be abolished.

U.S. Sen. Joseph S. Clark (D., Pa.) charged in August that "the people of Greece today live under an illegitimate military government." He proposed: "We as Democrats should pledge ourselves to work for the restoration of constitutional government in Greece by all appropriate peaceful means. To this end we should make plain our resolve to stop immediately all military assistance to the ruling junta and not to resume such assistance until democracy is re-established in Greece."

U.S. State Department officials disclosed Oct. 21 that the U.S. would resume the supply of major military equipment to Greece. American arms shipments had been suspended after the Apr. 1967 coup. The U.S. shipments, to begin with 2 minesweepers and 20 to 30 jet aircraft, were believed to have been resumed because of the U.S. government's desire to strengthen the southern flank of the NATO alliance.

GROWING RESISTANCE & JUNTA'S RESPONSE

Resistance to the military regime mounted during the following months and was manifested in many ways.

Papadopoulos Escapes Assassin

Premier George Papadopoulos was the target of an unsuccessful assassination attempt Aug. 13, 1968. A bomb exploded near his car on a coastal road 20 miles from Athens at 7:30 a.m. while the premier was on his way to his summer residence.

Police immediately arrested a suspect attempting to board a nearby boat. He was identified as Alexandros Panaghoulis, 30, who had deserted the army and had fled to Israel after the military regime had seized power in 1967. Panaghoulis had been repatriated by the Israeli authorities in Nov. 1967 but had escaped near Piraeus while returning to Greece. Panaghoulis confessed that he had sought to kill Papadopoulos to overthrow his regime and restore democracy in Greece.

Panaghoulis' seizure led to the arrest of 20 other suspects, the government announced Sept. 7. Athens charged that the assassination attempt had been planned by the Paris-based Greek Resistance Organization and engineered by Cypriot Interior & Defense Min. Polycarpos Georghiades and Andreas Papandreou, head of the Pan-Hellenic Liberation Movement, an anti-government organization based in Stockholm.

Panaghoulis and 14 others went on trial Nov. 4. Panaghoulis received 2 death sentences Nov. 17: one for having deserted the army while Greece was in a state of siege and another for a seditious attempt to overthrow the government. He also was given a 15-year prison term for attempted homicide and a 3-year sentence for illegal possession of arms. 8 other defendants received jail terms ranging from 2 1/2 years to life, 4 were acquitted and 2 received suspended sentences. Panaghoulis was ordered executed by firing squad within 72 hours of sentencing, but international pleas for clemency prompted a government stay of execution Nov. 21. The government Dec. 20 formally empowered the Justice Ministry to reprieve Panaghoulis. (Panaghoulis escaped from a military prison near Athens June 5, 1969 but was recaptured June 9, and 51 persons, including 4 army officers, were arrested in connection with his escape.)

Cypriot Interior & Defense Min. Georghiades resigned Nov. 1, 1968. His statement of resignation said that he was unable to continue his ministerial duties as a result of Greek government charges linking him to the assassination plot. (A Greek army intelligence officer had said at the Panaghoulis trial Nov. 4 that Georghiades had provided the explosives. Georghiades was later accused of complicity in an unsuccessful attempt to assassinate Cypriot Pres. Makarios Mar. 8, 1970, but he vehemently denied involvement in the plot. He then sought to leave Cyprus for what he described as "security reasons," but Cypriot police took him off a plane at Nicosia airport Mar. 13 as the aircraft was about to depart for Lebanon. Georghiades, 39, was found dead in his car Mar. 15, 1970 on a country road about 4 miles from Nicosia with 6 bullet holes in his chest. He reportedly had been lured to his death by a phone caller who had arranged a meeting on a promise to give him information on the attempt to slay Makarios.)

George Papandreou Dies

Ex-Premier George Papandreou, 80, died early Nov. 1, 1968, about 24 hours after surgery for a bleeding ulcer.

Papandreou had been a symbol of the World War II struggle for freedom in Greece. Born Feb. 13, 1888 in Kaledzi, a village near Patras in the Peloponnesus, the son of a local Greek Orthodox priest, Papandreou had studied law in Athens and political and economic sciences at the University of Berlin. On his return to Greece in 1915, Papandreou had become involved in anti-royalist politics, was elected to parliament and became interior minister in 1923. Exiled in 1926, he returned to serve in several governments before being exiled again in 1936 by the Metaxas dictatorship. Arrested by the Italians during the World War II occupation of Greece, he escaped and was premier of a government-in-exile 1944-5. Known as an anti-Communist, he served in several Social Democratic cabinets 1946-52, and in 1961 he formed the Center Union party. He was premier of Greece 1963-5.

Thousands of Greeks participated in Papandreou's funeral procession Nov. 3 and used the proceedings as a forum to demonstrate their opposition to the ruling military junta. The press around the world reported that more than 500,000 people lined the streets of Athens to view the casket of their dead leader. Even when Papandreou's body had been taken Nov. 1 from the hospital to Athens Cathedral, where it lay in state, crowds had lined the street and chanted "Pa-pan-dre-ou," a cry used in the ex-premier's political rallies. The regime had offered to give Papandreou, an opponent of the 1967 military coup and of the junta that has since ruled Greece, a state funeral. But Papandreou's family requested a private funeral.

As Papandreou's flag-draped coffin proceeded Nov. 3 on a 2-mile route to the cemetery, large crowds lined the streets and followed the procession. At Constitution Square in central Athens, about 50,000 persons defied martial-law rules against political rallies and chanted such slogans as "Pa-pan-dre-ou," "We want freedom," "You are still the premier" and "Down with tyranny." The crowd also shouted *"Oxi"*(no), a reference to the recent plebiscite, which had approved a new constitution presented by the junta. There were cries of: "This is the real plebiscite." The police did not interfere with the chanting crowd until a small group in the square started shouting "Out with the junta" and chanting the name of Andreas Papandreou, son of the late ex-premier, who was leading the anti-junta struggle from exile in Stockholm. Police charged the group, beat members of it and arrested several as other members of the crowd cried "Shame!"

Later Nov. 3 the military government announced that 40 persons had been arrested at the demonstration. 29 of them were sentenced by an Athens military court Nov. 6 to prison terms of 18 months to 4 years and 8 months for insulting the authorities and disobeying military orders.

A naturalized American citizen of Greek descent, Sam Alataris, was sentenced by the Athens military court Nov. 3 to a 2-year prison sentence for "insulting the Greek authorities." Alataris had shouted anti-junta slogans at the Papandreou funeral. (Alataris was released from prison Nov. 4, 1969 after having served one year of his sentence.)

Underground Warnings & Bombings

2 major Greek underground resistance organizations, Democratic Defence and the Patriotic Front, warned in a joint statement issued in Athens May 23, 1968 that "all foreign tourists who visit Greece will be considered as sympathizers who contribute directly or indirectly to the perpetuation of the dictatorship." "Consequently," the statement continued, "the resistance groups in Greece do not accept any responsibility for the safety of foreign tourists in Greece." The joint statement concluded by stating that "in the near future the Greek people will show that they are willing to fight openly against the military dictatorship and its foreign supporters."

A communique signed "Greek Resistance" threatened the Greek regime Aug. 16, 1968 with "increasingly more powerful actions." The communique, distributed to reporters in Athens, said Greek Resistance "will fight to final victory. It has the men, the organization, the power and the equipment to realize its promise and will not fail to prove it soon."

An anti-junta underground organization calling itself the Movement of National Resistance threatened in a statement issued July 29, 1969 to kidnap or kill U.S. personnel for alleged collaboration with the Greek military government. Copies of a handbill signed by "Gen. Akritas" and containing the threat on U.S. citizens were sent to foreign news agencies in Athens. The document was addressed to American "diplomats and double-crossers."

Foreign embassies and news agencies in Athens Sept. 22, 1969 received a press bulletin from the Greek Democratic Movement, another anti-government underground organization, reporting that it had set up "armed action groups."

Most of the underground activity reported consisted of bombings. *Among resistance actions reported:*
●At least 3 bombs exploded in Athens the evening of Oct. 24, 1968. The blasts broke shop windows and damaged a car. Police made several arrests.
●A bomb explosion the morning of Apr. 12, 1969 shattered windows in the building of the pro-junta Athens newspaper *Estia.*
●A commissary of a U.S. airbase in Greece and 2 American servicemen's cars were bombed May 18, 1969. Another explosion wrecked a U.S. Air Force member's car May 19.
●2 explosions damaged buildings and started a panic in Constitution Square May 19. The first bomb shattered windows in a branch office of the National Bank of Greece; the 2d exploded inside the building housing the offices of American Express and Litton Industries.
●The Athens Hilton was the scene of a bomb explosion May 22; nobody was reported injured.
●A bomb exploded at the entrance of an office building in Athens June 11 and injured 2 people.

●An undetonated time bomb was discovered July 23 in the U.S. Information Service library in Athens.

●A bomb explosion in Constitution Square July 26 injured 6 people, including two French tourists.

●8 American-owned autos were bombed in Athens suburbs July 28.

●A homemade bomb exploded outside the offices of the Northern Provinces Ministry in Salonika July 31. The only damage: shattered windowpanes.

●An explosion occurred in the headquarters of the Civil Servants' Union Aug. 3.

●Shortly after Demetrios Zafiropoulos, director general of press and information, had completed a news conference Aug. 3, a bomb exploded in the building where the conference had been held. No casualties were reported.

●An explosion Aug. 9 in the Olympic Airways office in Constitution Square injured 7 persons, 2 of them American tourists.

●A time-bomb exploded Sept. 13 in the offices of the pro-government Athens newspaper *Nea Politeia*. There were no casualties, but damage was described as extensive.

●2 more blasts caused damage at the City Hall and the neighboring central post office Sept. 22.

●A bomb exploded Sept. 28 in the basement of the new Palace of Justice in Larissa in central Greece.

●A small homemade bomb Oct. 7 damaged the car of Panayotis Makarezos, brother of the economic coordination minister. A spokesman for the Movement of National Resistance claimed responsibility for the blast.

●2 bombs exploded in front of the Galaxie Hotel on Academy Street in central Athens Oct. 13. The Greek Democratic Movement claimed responsibility for the act.

●8 bombs rocked Athens on Oct. 18; 6 pedestrians were injured and the trolley system was knocked out temporarily. The Public Order Ministry announced Oct. 23 that the men responsible for the Oct. 18 bombings had been arrested.

Police in Athens July 13, 1969 had discovered a work-shop used by opponents of the government for making bombs. The workshop was found in the home of a university professor, Dr. Dionysios Karagiorgas, after a bomb exploded accidentally there. The home was raided by the police after the blast. 4 Greek journalists were detained for questioning by security police July 16. Sources said their names were found, among several others, in a notebook kept by Karagiorgas. Those arrested were: Ioannis Kapsis, editor of the Athens newspaper *Ethnos;* George Tsapogas, financial reporter for the newspaper *Vima;* Demetrios Mortoyias, a junior reporter for *Vima,* and Miss Maria Kotzamani, an art critic. It was reported that 40 people were picked up in connection with the Karagiorgas affair. They included lawyers, journalists, bankers, and students. Prof. George Mangakis, a penal law expert, was arrested July 29 in connection with the Karagiorgas affair. Also arrested were Constantine Filias and Anthanasios Filias. The arrests were reported July 30. (Greek authorities asserted that Karagiorgas had told them he recalled having placed 2 bombs in Athens, one in front of a hotel, the other in front of a bank.)

Alexandros Archakis, a former Greek army captain, was given a 16-year prison sentence and Demetrios Lekkas, an electrician, received a 10 1/2-year sentence Oct. 20 on charges of having planted bombs in Athens Oct. 9.

At the end of October, 9 arrests were made in connection with recent bomb explosions. George Anomeritis, one of the defendants, was also accused of being a founder of the underground Greek Democratic Movement. The chief defendant was Demetrios Benas, a member of the Executive Council of the outlawed left-of-center party EDA. Benas was sentenced Nov. 5 to life imprisonment.

14 trials involving 43 defendants opened Oct. 29. Sentences of 8, 6 and 2 years in jail were imposed on 3 of the defendants on charges of possessing a suitcase full of explosives.

A special military tribunal Oct. 31 sentenced 8 defendants to prison terms ranging from 6 to 25 years in jail on charges of having planted time bombs in Athens.

A decree stiffening the penalties for bombings was made public Dec. 7. Life imprisonment was made mandatory for those found guilty of setting off explosives, and the penalty for explosions resulting in loss of life was life imprisonment or death.

Other Trials & Arrests

The Athens Special Military Court sentenced Lt. Gen. Archimidis Argyropoulos, 70, to a one-year suspended sentence Jan. 21, 1969 on charges of high treason. Argyropoulos, who had been arrested June 19, 1968, was accused of drawing up military plans, before the Apr. 1967 military coup, to be used "to alter the established regime of the country by violent means." Argyropoulos, who had been awarded the Order of the British Empire (OBE) and the U.S. Legion of Merit for his activities in World War II and the suppression of the Communist rebellion, pleaded that he had intended the plan "to meet possible disorder and rigging of elections and the protection of the legal regime."

An Athens military court Jan. 22 sentenced 2 persons to prison terms on charges of attempting to overthrow the military government through the illegal Patriotic Front, one of the underground groups plotting to overthrow the junta. Pavlos Nefeloudis, 45, a confessed Communist, was sentenced to life imprisonment, and Pericles Rodakis, 37, was jailed for 17 years.

Another Athens military court gave 3 students suspended sentences Jan. 22 and sentenced 2 others to 16 years in prison on charges of forming an illegal organization, Righas Ferraios, and plotting to overthrow the government.

An Athens court-martial Jan. 24 sentenced 3 men and a woman to 16 years' imprisonment for membership in the Patriotic Front. 3 of the 10 defendants were acquitted, and the others received less severe sentences.

An Athens military court sentenced Maj. Michael Avrameas, 42, to 14 months in prison Jan. 21 for dereliction of duty. Avrameas had played an important role in the 1967 coup but had supported King Constantine's abortive counter-coup in Dec. 1967. He was arrested early in 1968 on charges of embezzlement, extortion and forgery. The court found him not guilty of these charges but derelict in collecting part of his soldiers' pay to finance improved facilities for his unit.

A government list, published Feb. 19, deprived 24 expatriate Greeks, including 8 women, of their citizenship. The list included Anthony Ambatielos, 55, a former Greek Communist leader who had been sentenced to death in 1947 but pardoned and freed in 1964. He had fled to Britain after the 1967 coup.

An Athens court-martial Mar. 17 sentenced 3 persons to 5- and 10-year prison terms for plotting to overthrow the government. George Votsis, 33, a journalist living abroad, was sentenced in absentia to 5 years' imprisonment.

One of 16 Greeks charged with sedition claimed at his trial May 12 that he had been tortured by prosecution witnesses. Ioannis Nikolopoulos screamed at the Athens special military court: "They have tortured me. They smashed the door of my house and beat me up while I was in bed. My toenails still have pus from the torture."

An Athens military court May 14 convicted 16 persons on sedition charges and sentenced them to prison terms ranging from 8 months to life. Gregorios Farakos, 46, a member of the Politboro of the outlawed Greek Communist Party, was given life imprisonment.

A Salonika military court May 31 convicted 37 persons and sentenced them to terms ranging from 13 months' to life imprisonment on charges of plotting against the regime. 2 defendants were acquitted. The verdict brought the number of convictions on sedition charges to 125 in the past 3 weeks. The defendants, members of the leftist Patriotic Front, were charged with attempting to sabotage an electric plant at the Salonika Trade Fair in Sept. 1967 and with possession of arms and inciting the overthrow of the government.

A military court in Larissa, in central Greece, was reported May 21 to have sentenced 12 persons to prison terms of 3 to 20 years. They were accused of being members of the Patriotic Front.

A special military court in Athens May 23 sentenced economist Vassilios Filias to 18 years in prison on charges of sedition. He was accused of being a leader of the anti-junta Democratic Defense. Among 5 defendants convicted with Filias was novelist and ex-Judge Spyros Plaskovitis, who was sentenced to 5 years in prison. At his trial Filias said that "we who fight the present government do not consider ourselves as illegal, and that is why there is a legal basis for our right to resist." He added: "Moreover, the national crisis precipitated by the regime of 21 April requires the reconciliation of all Greeks, because the overthrow of the present catastrophic anomaly which threatens the foundations of our country constitutes the foremost national duty."

Mrs. Agheliki Mangakis, daughter of Stylianos Gonatas, who had been Greek premier 1922-4, was sentenced to 4 years in prison Aug. 27 for saying that her husband had been tortured by police. Mrs. Mangakis, 45, was charged with insulting the authorities and spreading false rumors. Her husband, George Mangakis, 47, a professor of law, had been arrested in July for interrogation in connection with a series of bomb explosions.

The government had announced Aug. 30 that it had dismantled a pro-royalist organization that had plotted to overthrow the regime and restore exiled King Constantine to his throne. Government press chief Demetrios Zaphiropoulos said that 50 persons, of whom 35 were military officers dismissed by the regime, had been arrested. Members of the leftist military organization Aspida were part of the organization, called Free Greeks, Zaphiropoulos said. Constantine Karamanlis, premier 1955-63, was named as an active and leading figure in the organization, along with Costas Coliyannis, leader of the Greek Communist Party. The press chief suggested that the organization was financed by foreign political parties. He said the German Social Democratic Party "might be one of them." Zaphiropoulos charged that the plotters had planted bombs in Athens during the summer to show their foreign backers that they were actively fighting the regime. Zaphiropoulos condemned Constantine for having failed to "energetically discourage" the plotters. The accusation was followed by a week-long anti-royalist campaign by Athens' 2 newspapers, *Eleftheros Kosmos* and *Nea Politeia.*

The announcement of the foiling of the alleged plot came 3 days after Constantine had flown to Switzerland to confer with Foreign Min. Panayiotis Pipinelis. The *N.Y. Times* reported Aug. 30 that the king had rejected Pipinelis' suggestion for his unconditional return to Greece and had insisted on 3 prerequisites: free elections under international supervision, full restoration of press freedom and the release of all persons arrested by the regime.

Yiannis Starakis, 28, a French journalist, was arrested in Athens Sept. 1. The French Union of Journalists (SNJ-CGT) protested "this new and serious blow committed by the Greek government to the universal right of freedom of information." The government asserted Oct. 1 that Starakis had been found in possession of 17 different passports and that he had been engaged in subversive activities in Greece.

The Athens military court Nov. 5 sentenced Nicolaos Anagnostopoulos to 20 years in prison and Charalambos Kalatzis to 15 on charges of subversive activities.

Students Margarita Yiarali and Kalliopi Tsempelikou, both 23, told an Athens military tribunal Nov. 3 that they had been tortured by security police. Both girls were on trial for subversion. Miss Yiarali, according to reports, told the tribunal: "I was brutally tortured so that I could not walk for months. I have been tortured by the police but they know ways to torture without leaving traces."

Christos Kondoyiorgos at his trial on Nov. 6 told the court that he had been beaten on the soles of his feet during interrogation at the Security Police Headquarters. The court then sentenced him to 20 years in prison on charges of sedition. A co-defendant, Stavros Sideris, 45, received a 16-year sentence.

Nicholas Anagnostopoulos, a former deputy of the right-wing National Radical Union, was reported arrested Nov. 15.

An Athens special court-martial Nov. 19 sentenced Maj. Anghelos Pnevmatikos to 5 years in prison for insulting the premier.

An Athens military tribunal Nov. 18 sentenced 7 people to prison terms of up to 8-1/2 years.

Lt. Col. Constantine Zissiou was sentenced Nov. 24 to 3 years' imprisonment by an Athens special military tribunal for allegedly engaging in anti-national propaganda. He was reported to have said that the Greek regime should have handed over power 3 months after the 1967 coup.

5 former Center Union deputies under house arrest had their terms extended for one year Nov. 27. The 5: John Papaspyrou, John Alevras, Constantine Koniatakis, John Charalambopoulos and Panayotis Katsikopoulos. Similar measures were taken against Antonios Levanis and George Katsipharas, former secretaries of Andreas Papandreou.

Ioannis Tsirimokos, a former left-wing member of parliament, was arrested Dec. 18 in Athens. No reason for the arrest was given.

Dissidents Flee to Exile

George Mylonas, former undersecretary of education, was reported Oct. 8 to have escaped from internment on the Aegean island of Amorgos. The escape, by cabin cruiser, was organized by 4 Italians, including Mario Scialoja, a correspondent for the weekly periodical *Espresso,* and one anti-government Greek resistance member. The Italians, posing as tourists on Amorgos, made contact with Mylonas and left with him by night in the boat. It was reported Oct. 16 that Mylonas, 50, had reached Geneva and had applied for (and later received) a Swiss residence permit. The *N.Y. Times* reported Oct. 11 that he planned to meet with all Greek leaders outside of Greece to try to bring about the unity necessary to overthrow the regime.

A Greek gunman Jan. 2 had commandeered an Olympic Airways DC-6B airliner, en route from Crete to Athens with 97 passengers and 5 crew members. He forced the pilot to fly the plane to Cairo and requested political asylum in the UAR. The hijacker, identified as George Paravolidakis (alias Flamouridis), 29, had ordered pilot Denis Mavrokefalous to fly to Cairo as the plane was taking off. When the pilot tried to contact airport authorities, Paravolidakis fired a shot over his head, shattering the flight deck window. Paravolidakis, who had served a prison sentence in Greece for violating martial law, said in Cairo that he was a Communist and planned eventually to go to Moscow. The plane returned to Athens empty the same day, and the passengers and crew flew back on another Olympic airliner.

Dr. and Mrs. Vassilios Tsironis, both armed with pistols, and their 2 young sons, armed with knives, hijacked an Olympic Airways DC-3 Aug. 16 and forced the pilot to land in Valona, Albania. Tsironis, 40, a physician who had been imprisoned by the government and placed on a list of persons not allowed to leave Greece, was granted political asylum in Albania. The plane, with its 24 remaining passengers and 3 crew members, all Greek, was returned to Greece Aug. 17. The aircraft, on a routine flight to Agrinion and Ioannina, had been intercepted in Albanian airspace by Albanian MIGs and ordered to land.

Olympic Airways Sept. 23 announced measures aimed at forestalling hijackings. Under the new regulations, tickets would be issued only on presentation of official identification.

Prisoners Released

Constantine Loundras, husband of Helen Vlachos, Athens publisher who had ceased publication of her 2 newspapers after the 1967 military coup, was discharged from prison Aug. 14, 1969 after serving 12 months for illegal possession of a revolver. Mrs. Vlachos had fled to England after escaping from house arrest in Athens. Loundras, recipient of the British Distinguished Service Cross, had been detained in Aug. 1968 following the attempt on Premier Papadopoulos' life. He had been sentenced in Oct. 1968 to 18 months in prison, but the Council of Pardons commuted the sentence to one year.

About 250 imprisoned Greeks whose sentences would have kept them in prison until Jan. 31, 1970 were released under a Christmas amnesty Dec. 17.

Military Purges

The government May 29, 1969 announced the arrest and banishment from Athens of 10 former senior military officers for "activities directed against public order, security and tranquility of the country." A Press Department statement said the ten would be "sent to exile to various parts of the country." All the arrested officers were regarded as royalists, and some had served as aides to exiled King Constantine. All had been retired or court-martialed after the army seized power in 1967. Government sources listed the officers as: Lt. Gen. Ioannis Gennimatis, former army chief of staff; Lt. Gen. Christos Papadatos, former commander for southern Greece; Lt. Gen. George Tsihlis, who was discharged for taking part in Constantine's abortive counter-coup in Dec. 1967; Maj. Gen. Constantine Papageorgiou, former military commandant of Athens; Brig. Gens. Demetrios Papadopoulos and Antonios Bouras; Navy Commodores Marios Stavridis and George Psallidas; and air force Col. Demetrios Papageorgiou and Lt. Col. Panayotis Diakoumakos.

The government June 21 announced the compulsory retirement or dishonorable discharge of 70 military officers. The ousters followed the unexplained dismissal June 20 of Gen. Pericles Malouhos, chief of the gendarmerie, and of Athens Police Chief Vassilios Sakellariou.

42 senior army officers, including 27 generals, were dismissed from their posts July 26 for allegedly "conspiring to topple the government and restore King Constantine" to power.

The London *Observer* of Jan. 11, 1970 reported that more than 3,000 people were then being held as political prisoners in Greece for periods of more than 2 years. Official Greek government statements maintained that only 1,800 to 1,900 were still detained.

INTELLECTUAL & POLITICAL DISSENT

Writers & Actresses Oppose Junta

George Seferis, the Greek poet who won the 1963 Nobel Prize for Literature, publicly attacked the Greek military regime Mar. 28, 1969. In a statement issued in Athens, Seferis said: "We have all learned that in dictatorial regimes the beginning may seem easy, yet tragedy lurks, inexorably, in the end. This abnormality must come to an end. It is the nation's command." Seferis said he had been moved to take a stand because of the junta's "state of enforced torpor in which all the intellectual values that we have succeeded ... in keeping alive, are being submerged in a swamp." The poet, who had been Greece's ambassador to London in the late 1950s, was accused by the Greek government "of being a Communist agent, intellectually barren and less worthy of the Nobel Prize than other more patriotic Greeks."

The *N.Y. Times* reported that 18 Greek writers had defied martial law Apr. 29 and denounced the Greek regime as illiberal and oppressive. In a signed statement they declared: "There can be no intellectual freedom ... as long as there is censorship which kills the fruitful exchange of ideas and restrains free and open communication." The signers of the declaration included Kay Cicellis, Alexandros Kotzias, Rodias Roufos and Costa Kaktsis.

In early May Anna Synodinou, one of Greece's foremost dramatic actresses, appealed to Greeks for action to help restore freedom to her country. Melina Mercouri, the Greek film star, and Michael Kakoyiannis, a film director, were reported in mid-July to have refused to go to the Moscow

Film Festival because the Russians had also invited representatives of the Greek government.

Political Groups Seek New Government

Nikitas Venizelos, grandson of the founder of the
Liberal Party, called May 4, 1969 for a unified national front
of all non-Communist Greek political forces under the leadership of Constantine Karamanlis, premier from 1955 to 1963.
Venizelos, 38, said that a coalition under Karamanlis was a
"realistic alternative" to the military regime. (Venizelos'
escape from Greece to Rome was reported by the London
Times Oct. 10. Venizelos, 39, had boycotted the Oct. 5
Athens ceremony unveiling a statue of his late grandfather,
Eleftheros Venizelos. He decried the "prevailing climate of
phobia, coercion and terror" that he ascribed to the junta's
actions. Venizelos had been forbidden to leave Greece, and his
passport had been confiscated in May at the Athens airport.)

It was announced July 27 that, under an agreement
reached between the Center Union and the National Radical
Union (ERE), the 2 parties intended to cooperate for either a
caretaker government, which would be able to replace the
junta, or a coalition government. The agreement stated that
those primarily responsible for the 1967 coup would be
brought to trial. The agreement was signed by ex-Economic
Coordination Min. George Mavros and ERE leader
Panayotis Kanellopoulos.

The underground Greek Democratic Movement disclosed in a proclamation issued Sept. 14 that it consisted of 5
major groups — the Democratic Union, Greek Resistance,
Philike Hetairia, Democratic Resistance and APFA — and
some smaller groups. Its proclamation demanded the replacement of the current regime by a caretaker government
consisting of all political parties. It also advocated the abolition of all laws imposed by the military regime and the
reinstatement of all purged officers. (The Greek Democratic
Movement Sept. 14 distributed leaflets warning athletes com-

peting in the European Games in Athens not to participate in celebrations sponsored by the junta.)

Democratic Defence, an underground organization, explained, in a document published in mid-September, its goals and plans. It said: "The correct strategy of the resistance...is...action which unites the people, action which convinces our people that something new is at last beginning. It is essential that we should in all circumstances seek for the experience of resistance to deepen the consciousness of the masses.... Our goal is the liberation of the Greek people."

Ex-Foreign Min. Evanghelos Averoff condemned the military regime July 20 and warned that the situation "will all end in chaos and bloodshed" unless the colonels restored normal political life to the country.

Junta Subjugates Administrative Judiciary

The Council of State, Greece's highest administrative tribunal, was defeated by the junta in a public clash during mid-1969 over the question of constitutional authority.

The confrontation took place after the council acted June 24 to cancel the dismissal of 21 of 30 magistrates purged by the government in May 1968. The government had acted against them with a constitutional amendment suspending their life tenure for 3 days. The amendment had provided for an inquiry prior to dismissal, but none was held. 21 of the magistrates had filed appeals to the council, set up 34 years previously to rule on the legality of government actions, and had won the appeals on the ground that they had not been able to defend themselves.

Premier Papadopoulos, denouncing the council's action as a *coup d'etat,* said he would ignore the decision and asked for the resignation of Michael Stasinopoulos, president of the council. Stasinopoulos, 66, refused to resign and was ousted June 27 by a decree nailed to the door of his home. Alexandros Dimitsas, 60, a council member, was appointed to the post. The vice president and 8 senior judges of the 25-man tribunal resigned in protest June 28 and were followed July 1 by 8 more council members.

Security police July 3 arrested one of the 21 reinstated judges and 3 lawyers who had defended them before the council. The 4 men were banished to remote villages for 6 months. Those exiled were public prosecutor Alexandros Floros and lawyers George Mangakis, Theoharis Zoukas, legal adviser to the late Premier George Papandreou, and Evanghelos Yiannopoulos. (Mangakis and Zoukas were released from exile Oct. 13 and were told they could resume work in Athens.)

The government July 4 introduced a law absolving itself of the constitutional obligation to accept the ruling delivered by the council June 24. The decree, retroactive to June 1, stated that the "decisions of any tribunal, issued on any case exempted from its jurisdiction, are non-existent and not to be enforced."

Demetrios Papaspyrou, the last president of Greece's defunct Parliament, was reported by the *N.Y. Times* July 9 to have issued a statement criticizing the government's actions against the judiciary. Papaspyrou, a former justice minister, appealed to foreign jurists to lend moral support to opponents of the regime.

(The government July 1 had named Gen. Spyros Veliantitis, general director of national security, as ombudsman "to defend the rights of Greek citizens against bureaucracy.")

TORTURE OF PRISONERS CHARGED

Look & Harper's Magazines Report Atrocities

Christopher Wren, senior editor of *Look* magazine, reported in a May 27, 1969 article entitled "Greece: Government by Torture": "The reports of torture filtering out of Greece for 2 years since the military coup were so grotesque as to seem unreal. It took a trip inside Greece to change my mind. A succession of former political prisoners described every ordeal of torture in detail and let me see, and touch, the scars. Now I am convinced torture has taken place in Greece on victims who number into the thousands. Under a frightened, unpopular military regime, torture goes on today."

Wren's article described the ordeal of Pericles Korovessis, 28, an Athens actor: "5 armed plainclothesmen burst into his apartment. They took Pericles in an unmarked black sedan down to police headquarters. They took him into a small room.... In the middle was a wooden bench. They tied him down on it.... One man held his chest...another picked up a shovel handle. He began pounding Korovessis on the soles of his dangling feet. With a stick...a soaked rag was jammed inside of his mouth. When he came to they started on his feet again."

The Greek embassy in Washington issued a press release categorically rejecting "the slanderous and totally foundless allegations contained in the [Wren] article." The release concluded by stating that "this article and the emotional way in which it was presented serves more the purpose of sensationalism than the cause of truth." It quoted Premier

Papadopoulos as saying that he would personally and publically execute, in Constitution Square, anyone proven to have administered torture.

In an article entitled "Greece: The Death of Liberty" in the Oct. 1969 issue of *Harper's* magazine, John Corry related the experiences of a number of people who claimed that they had been tortured by the Greek government. Among those interviewed by Corry were Nikolaos Kiaos, 26, a student, and Athanasios Kanellopoulos, 31, a telephone company employe. Kiaos charged that he had been beaten in the General Asfalia police station: "For a long while he [a police officer] was beating my head on the wall. They beat me on the soles of my feet with iron and wooden rods. They beat me on my genitals." Corry quoted Kanellopoulos as saying: He had been arrested Jan. 1, 1969. "I was led straight to a colonel, ... who beat me for 2 solid hours. I was then handed over to the Piraeus Security Police, where I was beaten incessantly for 10 days on the soles of my feet. The most severe blows I received on my testicles by kicking."

James Beckett, who investigated tortures in Greece for Amnesty International (London) in 1968, asserted Oct. 12, 1969 that Yiannis Papatakis, commandant of the Naval Cadets School in Greece (but currently in Brussels with NATO), had told him that "torture is necessary to defend our civilization."

Rights Unit Calls Torture a Policy

A confidential report prepared by the European Commission on Human Rights concluded "beyond doubt" that the Greek regime practiced torture as a matter of policy and denied fundamental human rights to Greek citizens. The report also asserted that no Communist threat had existed at the time of the 1967 coup as the junta had contended. The commission, an agency of the 18-nation Council of Europe, presented its findings to the council's member nations Nov. 18 in a 4-volume, 1,200-page study. 8 international lawyers had spent 2 years in the investigation, interrogating 87 witnesses. They were joined by 7 more lawyers in the evaluation of the evidence, which had been collected on the basis of charges brought against Greece in 1967 by Sweden, Denmark, Norway and the Netherlands.

The report listed 213 cases in which there was *prima facie* evidence of torture. It produced evidence strongly suggesting that 5 men, who were identified, had died as a result of torture. The report alleged that a member of the junta, Ioannis Ladas, had personally tortured one prisoner. The most common form of torture was *falanga,* a severe beating with wooden or metal rods. The commission found that the "acts of torture or ill-treatment are not isolated or exceptional, nor limited to one place" and that the practice of torture had become an "administrative practice" that was "officially tolerated." Competent Greek authorities, according to the report, had failed to take any steps to investigate or remedy complaints of torture though "confronted with numerous and substantial . . . allegations."

(A report on alleged police torture of 15 women political prisoners had been smuggled out of Greece July 1 by a Danish woman for presentation to the commission.)

About half of the report dealt with the defense presented by the junta in justification of the suspension of civil liberties in Greece. The junta maintained that left-wing groups had been planning violent revolution before the coup that brought the colonels to power. The commission concluded that there was considerable evidence that no such plans existed. A Communist takeover "was neither planned at that time nor seriously anticipated by either the military or police authorities," the commission said. The junta had produced a letter charging that the late George Papandreou, leader of the Center Union party, had been in negotiation with the Communists. The commission held that one of the junta's own witnesses had proved the letter to be a forgery.

The report concluded that the Greek regime was in clear violation of Article 3 of the Council of Europe's charter. That article stated that members must guarantee the "principles of the rule of law" and "human rights and fundamental freedoms."

Constantine Panayotacos, Greece's representative to the Council, Nov. 30 described the commission report as "shocking and deplorable." In Athens Dec. 1, Economic Coordination Min. Nikolaos Makarezos warned envoys from Britain, West Germany, Italy, Belgium, Holland, Denmark and Norway that Greece would apply economic sanctions against nations that pressed for Greece's expulsion from the Council of Europe. Meanwhile, Foreign Office officials in Britain, which was leading the movement to expel Greece, met in London Dec. 4 with the ambassadors of Denmark, Norway and Sweden to solidify the position against Greece. Greek Foreign Min. Panayotis Pipinelis flew to Paris Dec. 7 to attempt to block the movement to oust Greece from the Council. (Pipinelis received a representative of the International Red Cross Oct. 23 and reportedly agreed to allow Red Cross representatives to visit civilian and military camps and prisons.)

INTERNATIONAL DEVELOPMENTS

Council of Europe Threatens Expulsion

Dr. Max van der Stoel, the Council of Europe's representative for Greek affairs, reported Jan. 20, 1969 to the Consultative Assembly of the Council of Europe that "the atmosphere of intimidation and of silent terror [in Greece] does not seem to have changed within the last few months. All political activity and political propaganda other than from the government or following the official line of the regime is either forbidden or practically impossible."

Van der Stoel concluded with these remarks: "The [Consultative] Assembly has shown considerable patience towards Greece, which has ceased to fulfill the conditions for membership in the Council of Europe. Now the time has come to draw the consequences from this situation. It is undeniable that the present Greek regime does not fulfill the objective conditions for membership in the Council of Europe. . . . Greece must in consequence forego the benefits of membership in the Council."

After hearing van der Stoel's report, the Assembly voted 92-14 Jan. 30 to recommend to the Committee of Ministers of the Council of Europe the suspension of the Greek government from the Council of Europe. Van der Stoel said Nov. 23, 1969 that this decision had been reached because "virtually none of the promises [of the Greek government] had really been lived up to; . . . they were not implemented; and there was no visible progress of Greece towards democracy."

The Committee of Ministers of the Council of Europe warned the Greek government May 6, 1969 that its internal policies violated the principles of human rights on which the Council was founded. The Committee approved by 13-2 vote (with 3 abstentions) a 4-point resolution warning Greece that it was in danger of expulsion from the Council. Greece and Cyprus voted against the resolution, and France, Switzerland and Turkey abstained.

(The Greek Foreign Ministry, evidently authorized by King Constantine, Nov. 24 issued a statement denying press reports that the king had been soliciting the support of European governments for Greece's expulsion from the Council of Europe. The original press report had been made Nov. 18 by the Copenhagen newspaper *Politiken,* which said Constantine, while visiting Britain, had urged various government contacts Nov. 14 to work for Greece's expulsion.)

European Parliament Urges Restoration of Democracy

The European Parliament May 7, 1969 passed a resolution stating that "the association agreement [between Greece and the European Economic Community] cannot be fully applied until a democratic, parliamentary regime has been restored in Greece, and that there can be no question of subsequent membership in such conditions."

The European Parliament, responsible for the operation of the EEC and other European Community institutions, appealed for the immediate repeal of repressive measures in Greece and warned that "in the absence of any development in the direction indicated, it reserves the right to take steps to have the association agreement revised or suspended." Finally, the European Parliament expressed the hope that "the governments of the countries of the European Community will take due heed of the present resolution both with regard to the attitude they adopt in the Council of Ministers of the Community and in their bilateral relations with Greece."

NATO Condemns Greece

The Plenum of the Parliamentary Assembly of NATO voted 26-4 (with 2 abstentions) Oct. 20, 1969 to condemn Greece for its denials of democratic rights. The resolution urged "the governments of the other 14 members of the alliance to utilize all appropriate means to bring about, promptly, a return by Greece to free elections, parliamentary democracy and the rule of law and to concert their actions in this respect."

Erich Blumenfeld of West Germany told the NATO Assembly "that the government of Athens should in a very, very short time realize that our patience with all that took place and that still takes place in Greece has its limits." U.S. Sen. Jacob Javits (R., N.Y.), chairman of the Political Committee of the Parliamentary Assembly of NATO, said that Greek politicians in exile should be called before the next meeting of the NATO Assembly.

31 members of the last Greek parliament, in a joint declaration, hailed the NATO Parliamentary Assembly's denunciation of the junta. The signatories said that it was consoling to see that the NATO parliamentarians had not forgotten that "a small but proud people of the alliance had been brutally deprived of its elementary civil and political liberties."

U.S. Action

An American cargo vessel delivered 5 F-104 Starfighter jets to Greece Feb. 17, 1969. This was the first major U.S. military aid delivered to Greece in 22 months. The jets were the last of a 3-year-old aid consignment.

50 members of the U.S. Congress had written to State Secy. William Rogers July 30 to indicate their concern over events in Greece. The letter stated that "the sooner the junta

falls, the greater the prospect that a responsible, democratic, Western-oriented successor government will emerge to bind the economic and political wounds." The Congress members urged "that a clearer sign of U.S. moral and political disapproval of the dictatorship be given and sustained...[and] that U.S. military aid to Greece should not be increased and, indeed, should be curtailed."

The letter was signed by: Joseph P. Addabbo, Glenn M. Anderson, Jonathan Bingham, John Brademas, George E. Brown Jr., Phillip Burton, Shirley Chisholm, Jeffery Cohelan, John Conyers Jr., James Corman, R. Lawrence Coughlin, Charles C. Diggs Jr., Donald Edwards, Joshua Eilberg, Donald M. Fraser, Jacob Gilbert, Seymour Halpern, Augustus Hawkins, Henry Helstoski, Floyd Hicks, Daniel Inouye, Charles Joelson, Robert Kastenmeier, Edward Koch, Robert Leggett, Allard Lowenstein, Abner Mikva, Patsy Mink, William S. Moorhead, John Moss, Lucien Nedzi, Gaylord Nelson, Robert N. C. Nix, Richard Ottinger, Bertram L. Podell, Adam C. Powell, Thomas Rees, Ogden R. Reid, Henry Reuss, Peter Rodino Jr., Benjamin Rosenthal, Edward Roybal, William F. Ryan, William L. St. Onge, James Scheuer, Louis Stokes, Frank Thompson Jr., Jerome R. Waldie, Stephen M. Young.

William B. Macomber Jr., Assistant State Secretary for Congressional relations, replying to the Congress members on Rogers' behalf, said: "We, in the State Department, see an autocratic government denying basic civil liberties to the citizens of Greece. We think such an internal order does not coincide with the best interests of Greece. Our policy on military assistance has been motivated by our desire to see Greece evolve towards representative government. Our dilemma is how to deal with an ally whose internal order we disagree with yet who is a loyal NATO partner."

U.S. Rep. Donald Edwards (D., Calif.), chairman of the U.S. Committee for Democracy in Greece, said Oct. 26 that "the Nixon Administration policy insofar as the State Department is concerned is not too satisfactory. Our military really props up the military government in Greece, it supports it publicly." U.S. Rep. Edward Koch (D., N.Y.) said Oct. 29 that "we can ill afford to continue our tacit approval for this outrageously tyrannical government which despite its protestations for future democratic reform makes no visible effort in that direction."

Rep. Edwards' office reported in a press release Nov. 25 that "a claim by the Greek military dictatorship that the United States is considering a step-up in military aid has led 27 [U.S.] Congressmen to urge Pres. Nixon to stop all military shipments" to Greece. The press release said that the 27 Congress members "respectfully urge that the United States make clear its moral disapproval of the present Greek government, and we further urge that all United States military aid to that nation be discontinued."

The U.S. Senate overrode the recommendation of its Senate Foreign Relations Committee and voted Dec. 12 to restore full arms aid to Greece.

Pres. Nixon Aug. 24 had appointed Henry Tasca, U.S. ambassador to Morocco, as ambassador to Greece. The appointment was confirmed by the Senate Dec. 20 after a 4-month delay. Sen. Charles Goodell (R., N.Y.) had delayed Senate confirmation Dec. 11 as "an additional signal of our displeasure with the Greek dictatorship's present practices." The delay, Goodell said, would also serve to "encourage responsible elements in Greece to press for more democratic and humane policies."

Exiled opposition leader Andreas Papandreou had charged June 18 that the U.S. and NATO were the sole sources of strength of the Greek junta. Papandreou said at a London meeting of the Socialist International Congress that American support of the regime guaranteed the U.S. Navy access to the Mediterranean in case of a Soviet fleet build-up there. Papandreou had claimed May 20 that the CIA had been aware that Greek agents knew of exiled King Constantine's abortive plans for a countercoup but that the CIA did not inform the king because of U.S. support for the junta.

Italian Leader Aids Andreas Papandreou

Relations between Greece and Italy were strained by reports Mar. 7 that Italian Foreign Min. Pietro Nenni had promised his Socialist Party's support to Andreas Papandreou. Papandreou had visited Rome Mar. 5 at the invitation of the Socialist Party, a partner in the Italian coalition government. It was reported Mar. 7 that Italian Socialists had pledged to coordinate their actions with Papandreou's movement and step up pressure on the Greek government "to restore the people's sovereignty."

Greek Premier Papadopoulos said Mar. 15 that Nenni could not say one thing as a party leader and another as foreign minister of a country with which Greece maintained friendly relations, cooperated in a defense alliance and shared common objectives. According to a Mar. 24 report, the Greek government had decided to impose a selective boycott of Italian goods if Italy refused to make public amends for "hostile remarks" by Nenni. Foreign Min. Pipinelis said Italy's explanation of the remarks had been inadequate.

Radio, TV & Press Activity

The Greek regime ordered a special investigation of British Broadcasting Corp. broadcasts modeled on code messages transmitted to resistance fighters during World War II, and a junta spokesman said Aug. 6, 1969 that protests would be made to the British government if it were established that the messages were directed to anti-regime groups in Greece. The messages were broadcast on the evening Greek-language program Aug. 4 and 5; they were preceded and followed by the wartime identification signal — the first 4 bars of Beethoven's *5th Symphony*. No explanation was given at the time of the broadcasts, but the BBC announcer said Aug. 6 that the messages "had no significance at all" and were part of the forthcoming 30th anniversary celebration Sept. 30 of the BBC Greek news service. (The Greek service of the BBC increased its broadcasts to Greece right after the 1967 coup and maintained an editorial policy critical of the regime.)

An anti-junta radio program entitled "Deutsche Welle" began broadcasting from Cologne, Germany to Greece in 1968. In Dec. 1968 "The Free Voice of Greece," an anti-junta program of news and commentary, began broadcasting in Greek and English to a N.Y. City audience. "The Greek Hour," a TV program on a UHF station in the N.Y. City area, presented programs that often supported the Greek junta. *Greek Report,* an anti-junta monthly journal of information and documents about Greek affairs, began publication in London in Feb. 1969. Several anti-junta journals in Greek and other languages appeared in Canada and various European cities.

New Press Regulations

The government Apr. 7 ordered all newspapers except the conservative Athens daily *Estia* to devote an entire page in every weekend edition, beginning Apr. 13, to excerpts from a new "State Anthology of Modern Greek Letters." The newspapers were ordered to continue the practice for 2-1/2 years. The government announcement stressed that the anthology was free from censorship and included among its 86 authors "9 self-confessed Communists, 9 leftists" and other opponents of the regime.

A government decree June 23 authorized additional pages to newspapers that "help raise the people's spiritual and moral standards." Greece had rationed imported newsprint for 24 years to improve its foreign exchange position. Dailies had been permitted a total of 112 pages every 2 weeks. A 3-man panel was to determine which newspapers qualified for the new privilege. Greece abolished press privileges Nov. 16 by instituting a new press law ending exemptions for imported newsprint. The new law did not affect newspapers with a circulation of under 25,000 daily. *Acropolis, Apogevmatini* and *Ta Nea,* 3 newspapers recently criticized by the government, had a higher circulation than 25,000 and were affected by the new law. The government announced that the new law was meant to "cleanse and discipline" the press.

2 pro-government newspapers — *Eleftheros Kosmos* and *Nea Politeia* — joined the 600-member Union of Athens Journalists Aug. 23, 1969 in an attack on the 180-article

press law draft. The union's statement said the press law was "inadmissible and objectionable." The law provided severe penalties for publishing reports aimed at overthrowing the regime or insults against Christianity, the king or the government. It would establish a "registration" system under which only registered and approved journalists would be able to work. The press law went into effect Jan. 1, 1970. Deputy Premier Pattakos stated Jan. 1 that the press law held severe penalties because "Severity is the mother of justice and freedom."

Premier Papadopoulos Oct. 3, 1969 abolished pre-censorship of newspapers and said a new press code would be promulgated before mid-November. The order, which went into effect immediately, proclaimed that "the publication of information, news and comments through the press is free," but articles criticizing the 1967 coup or creating doubts about the economy, public order, security and the armed forces were still banned. The Athens daily *To Vima* Oct. 5 rejected the regime's lifting of press controls as inadequate and said it would refuse to resume publication of political editorials until "all political and individual liberties" were restored.

Officials warned newsmen Oct. 7 to exercise discretion or face trial under martial law.

Restoration of Rights Claimed

The junta decreed Apr. 9, 1969 that 3 constitutional rights, held in abeyance since the new constitution came into effect Nov. 15, 1968, were to be restored immediately: the inviolability of citizens' homes, the right of association and the right of assembly. 9 other constitutional rights remained suspended, and martial law was still in force.

Announcing the move, Premier Papadopoulos outlined other liberalizing measures that were to be immediately implemented. These included: (1) All civil servants except those of high rank who had been dismissed as opponents of the regime could be reinstated after review through normal channels; (2) judicial commissions would be set up to review the cases of nearly 2,000 persons who were still being held in exile on Aegean islands; (3) a new press code fixing methods of censorship and qualifications for journalists was put into effect. Papadopoulos also announced that 18 commissions of jurists had been set up to draft legislation to implement the new constitution. 2 of these commissions were to work on laws governing the rights of assembly and association, and it was unclear how these rights were to be protected in the absence of the legislation.

In anticipation of the 2d anniversary of the military coup, Papadopoulos announced Apr. 19 that the "democracy" being constructed by the junta "will henceforth constitute the permanent framework for the activities and development of the Greek nation." He warned "the deserters who are scheming abroad and the few at home who share their hopes" that they would "find themselves permanently on the margin of national life."

Demetrios Papaspyrou, president of the Parliament dissolved shortly before the 1967 coup, charged Apr. 11 that the restoration of limited rights changed nothing and was designed to "create a false impression."

Conditions for possible cooperation with civilian politicians were outlined May 25 in an article in *Nea Politeia* (New State), an Athens daily that reportedly reflected the personal views of Papadopoulos. The article said: "If the former politicians...wish to serve and to help in the rapid restoration of normal political life, they must fulfill at least 3 basic conditions: recognize that the revolution was necessary and has made a positive contribution; repudiate unequivocally the frantic extremists; endorse the radical institutional reforms carried out in the context of the new constitution."

Deputy Premier Pattakos had declined Apr. 25 to set a time limit for the country's return to democratic rule. Pattakos said the military regime had enough work to keep it busy and in power for a long time to come.

Papadopoulos stated Sept. 6, at the opening of the Salonika Trade Fair, that "the goal of our National Revolution is...to regroup all the living forces and bind them together for a great leap forward in the economic and social sectors. This leap can not be achieved under parliamentary rule."

Papadopolous Oct. 3 announced guarantees of personal liberty except in cases involving crimes against public order and security. He also announced a new limitation on the jurisdiction of special military courts.

A decree issued in mid-Dec. 1969 stiffened the penalties for "rumor-mongering." The decree made it a punishable offense to disseminate or publish false information or rumors likely to undermine public confidence in the state, in its domestic and foreign investment policies or in tourism.

(A new "code of behavior" for university students, scheduled to take effect when martial law was lifted, was decreed Jan. 27, 1969. The code provided punishment ranging from warnings to lifetime expulsion from school for students who disobeyed university rules, disturbed the peace, participated in student strikes or showed disrespect of university authorities. Martial law was still in force as of Apr. 1970.)

Junta Curbs Strikes

The Greek government decreed a series of curbs on labor unions on May 10, 1969 in an effort to deter strikes and discourage employment of career unionists as leaders. According to the decrees, courts may disband any union or dismiss any labor leader whose activities "are directed against the established political system and social order, state security and territorial integrity as well as the political or individual freedoms of citizens." The new legislation ordered the dismissal from paid union posts of all officials who had not held outside employment for at least 600 days in the 6 years prior to their election. It was estimated that 100 union leaders would lose their positions as a result of the law.

Prison Developments

The government Sept. 18 announced plans to build 3 new prisons in Salonika, Larissa and Patras, each to hold 360 prisoners.

Political prisoners on Leros Island appealed Jan. 2, 1970 for medical care and the release of "the seriously ill, the invalid and the aged." In a statement sent to foreign news agencies, the prisoners at Lakki, Greece's largest detention camp, said 684 of the 1,050 held were suffering from influenza and that one person had died in the epidemic.

Political prisoners in Kordallos prison in Piraeus and Averoff prison in Athens announced Jan. 13, 1970 that they had begun a hunger strike to protest the death of the prisoner at Lakki detention camp.

Censorship of Movies & Theater

The government decreed July 26, 1969 that all movies shown at festivals in Greece and all Greek film entries in festivals abroad must be "compatible with the religious beliefs and the traditions of the Greek people [and with] public order and national security."

It was reported Aug. 8 that all further performances of the ancient Greek tragedy *Electra,* by Euripides, had been banned from Greek festivals for 1969 because some of the costumes designed for the play were deemed to be "un-Greek."

Economic Developments

The *Wall Street Journal* reported June 12, 1969 that the First National City Bank of New York would aid in financing the construction of a 55-mile highway in northern

Greece. The bank agreed to lend $10 million to a private Greek company for the project.

An agreement signed with the Soviet Union in mid-Dec. 1969 provided for Soviet aid in planning and erecting an electrical plant to be built in Macedonia. A decision by the Greek government to admit Soviet goods at reduced tariffs was made public Jan. 20, 1970.

It was disclosed the week of Jan. 17, 1970 that a delegation of the Greek Chamber of Commerce would go to East Germany to renew a trade agreement and to negotiate the possibility of establishing a permanent Greek trade mission in East Berlin.

The Greek government Jan. 22, 1970 awarded to the Soviet Union rights to conduct a peat survey near Philippi, northwest of the port of Kavalla in northern Greece in a plan to produce electric power. This area was a frequent site for NATO maneuvers. Previous Greek governments had refused to allow Soviet technicians to move freely in the militarily vulnerable area separating Bulgaria and Greece. (The Greek government said Jan. 24, 1970 that it intended to begin negotiations for a renewal of trade between Greece and Bulgaria.)

The Greek regime announced Jan. 24, 1970 that it had concluded an agreement with Albania to resume trade relations, which were broken 30 years ago. The agreement was signed in Paris after a week of negotiations. These developments were seen by many observers as a reaction to mounting Western criticism of the junta.

Shortly before Christmas 1969 the Greek government awarded an exclusive contract for the establishment of a vast automobile complex to 2 Italians and one Greek, none of them known as automobile manufacturers. The decree awarding the contract stated that the investors would have a 6-year exclusive contract for the manufacture of automobiles, lorries, farm and road construction vehicles and engines in return for pledges to provide a bank guarantee by Feb. 1970, and to import $60 million in cash and loans, or equivalent value in parts and machinery, over an 8-year period. (The Athens newspaper *Estia* called on the regime to clarify its reasons for awarding this contract without international competition.)

The Greek government Oct. 14, 1969 cancelled a 12-year multimillion-dollar management contract with Litton-Greece, a subsidiary of Litton Industries, Inc., because of its failure to secure adequate foreign financing for Greek economic development projects. The contract had been scheduled for revision in May, at which time Litton was committed to be engaged in projects involving investments of at least $120 million. Litton's failure to meet this commitment resulted in negotiations focused on shrinking the scope of the contract. The talks collapsed Oct. 14.

In an effort to improve the balance of international payments, the government took steps during 1969 to try to increase exports, curb imports and reverse the decline in tourism that had followed the military takeover. The regime was reported Sept. 28 to have tried to make visits to Greece more attractive to Greeks living abroad by exempting them from army draft obligations. It was reported Aug. 10 to have made an additional move in trying to close the widening trade gap by ordering an investigation of all import invoices before they were approved.

In its year-end review of European economic affairs, the *N.Y. Times* Jan. 16, 1970 wrote: "The Greek government is borrowing heavily abroad to keep its delicate balance of payments on an even keel. Imported business capital in 1969 was in the range of $150 million." Since 1966 "the Greek foreign trade deficit has soared by more than $100 million."

The Greek government's 1970 budget included a 5% raise for State employes and a similar raise for pensioners. The 1970 budget also allocated $431.4 million for economic development and $426.4 million for defense and internal security.

Economic Claims Disputed

A group of liberal and conservative former politicians Aug. 3, 1969 issued a survey challenging the regime's claim that the national finances were in better shape than ever before. The 16-page report, released on behalf of the group by former Commerce Min. Emmanuel Kothris, called for prompt restoration of democracy to avert serious economic trouble. The report cited the doubling of defense outlays since 1966, the 170% increase in the government's debt to the Bank of Greece and the rise in national income of only 24% in the past 3 years based on current prices.

John Pesmazoglu, a former deputy governor of the Bank of Greece, defied martial law in mid-October and accused the government of keeping certain economic information from its people. Pesmazoglu asserted that a slowdown in economic growth rates could be observed since 1967. The growth rate of the GNP in 1967 and 1968, he said, was 4.4% as against 7.6% in the 4 years before the coup. He pointed out that the balance-of-payments deficit had soared under the junta and that the gap was being met by foreign credits.

The London *Financial Times* reported Aug. 22, 1969 that reports of a serious foreign exchange constraint might "make it necessary [for the government] to introduce policies designed to promote exports and control the expansion of imports." The World Bank Economic Committee released a report that stated that such policies might include increasing productivity or slowing down the increase in demand, particularly for consumer goods.

The *Economist* reported Nov. 7 that Greece's "external obligations are around $1,870 million and rising fast to subsidize a weak balance of payments." In terms of foreign investments, the magazine stated that "in the first 8 months of 1969 the inflow was $89 million, still below 1968, while the cost of servicing foreign debts rose to $50 million, compared with $11 million in the same period of 1966. Balance of payments deficit was $230 million, against $120 million by the end of Aug. 1966."

KARAMANLIS' CALL FOR JUNTA'S OVERTHROW

Ex-Premier Offers to Head Interim Regime

Ex-Premier Constantine Karamanlis, in a statement issued Sept. 30, 1969, appealed to his country's military forces to overthrow the army-backed regime. He expressed willingness to head an interim government following the departure of the junta. Karamanlis, 62, founder of the conservative National Radical Union, had been living in Paris since his defeat in 1963 by the Center Union party. He had been premier 1955-63. The statement, his first public one since 1967, was not reported by the Greek press. Karamanlis charged that the junta had disrupted the armed forces, undermined the economic future of the country and isolated Greece politically and morally from the family of free nations.

Support for Karamanlis was expressed by ex-Premier Panayotis Kanellopoulos, leader of the National Radical Union, and by Demetrios Papaspyrou, president of the last Greek parliament before the 1967 coup. The left-of-center anti-government Democratic Defense organization also hailed the Karamanlis statement. Qualified support came from Andreas Papandreou, son of late Center Union leader George Papandreou.

At a news conference Oct. 4, Economic Coordination Min. Nikolaos Makarezos termed Karamanlis' charges "irresponsible." Makarezos said that it was not the Greek economy that was at stake but Karamanlis' own political future. (It was reported that following the Karamanlis declaration military units in Greece had been placed on alert and that some army commanders in the north had been replaced.)

115

In his statement, issued in Paris, Karamanlis said:

"It is now one year since the famous plebiscite and, instead of making progress, the cause of democracy in Greece has moved dangerously backwards. The government has become more tyrannical and now identifies itself with democracy in the most cynical possible manner. Arbitrary rule has now become entrenched and the despairing opposition of the people has reached new heights.

"In this situation I feel obliged once again to break my silence and to call attention to the serious dangers which threaten the country by the continuation of the present abnormality.

"As I said on a previous occasion, the military government of Athens made an additional mistake from the very beginning: their determination to create a situation of permanency. But, lacking the courage to make this purpose openly known, they attempted to conceal it by their clumsy claims to be the flag-bearers of democracy. And by this contradictory and unreasoned policy they have created a tyrannical and illegitimate regime in which both the government and the country are rotting away. For the Athens regime, lacking among other things any clear ideological orientation, conforms to no kind of political pattern or purpose — not even that of the classical form of dictatorship. . . .

"As a result of this initial mistake, the government has made a whole series of further mistakes. Thus:

"1. It has dismembered the armed forces of Greece by subjecting them to a process of Sovietization and by the dismissal of hundreds of high-ranking, battle-experienced officers who might have hindered their objectives.

"2. It has continued in an even more acute form the demagogic policies of its predecessors, thereby undermining the economic future of the country, increasing without a care consumer expenditures at the expense of investment, widening the balance-of-payments gap (making good the deficiency by borrowing on the most onerous terms), and, finally, permitting an enormous increase in the country's foreign exchange debt, now estimated at $1,870 million, of which $420 millions are in the form of short-term commercial credits. . . .

"3. It has isolated the country politically and morally. Greece, nucleus of the European spirit, is now being pushed out of the family of free nations. And to appreciate the full significance of this isolation, we must bear in mind the critical geopolitical position of our country and the fact that Greece will find herself excluded from the European groupings which are now taking shape, to the detriment not only of her economy but of her national security.

"Finally, by their tyrannical rule, their idle boasting and their hit-or-miss methods, they have created an explosive situation in Greece and deprived Greece of any international repute.

"Worst of all, the government clings to its initial error and, instead of searching for a solution of the problem, seeks ways and means to ensure the indefinite continuation of the present regime. Until recently, it believed it could succeed by an electoral coup. Indeed, it went in search of collaborators for that purpose. Now it seeks the same objectives by terrorization of the Greek people and by hoodwinking international public opinion.

"And the government clings to its errors because it does not realize that, if the reactions against it — both domestic and international — have so far been of a moderate nature, it is because of the expectations that were created by the repeated assurances it gave about the restoration of democracy. But the deception is now plain for all to see, and the government, under the pressure of the gathering storm, will be forced to make a choice. . . .

" . . . The whole future of the Greek nation will be profoundly influenced by the decision to be taken in the next few months. It is vital that these decisions should be the right ones. Otherwise Greece will suffer evil days without end.

"Some 2 years ago, at another critical moment for the nation, I made public my views about the political problem of Greece. I condemned the past, expressed my anxiety about the present, and sketched out a course for the future. At that time, I said, among other things:

" 'The present troubled situation gives rise to the need, and at the same time presents the opportunity, to re-shape democracy in Greece. The present government must therefore give way to an experienced and strong government which, exercising special powers, and within a reasonable period of time, will create conditions which will permit the functioning of democracy in Greece and allow the country to go forward in safety.'

"I would counsel the government, now that it has more experience, to study my proposals before the impasse becomes impenetrable both for itself and the country. I believe that those proposals not only facilitate the safe restoration of democracy but the foundation of a new and healthy political life which will combine freedom with order and progress with social justice. . . .

"Under conditions as they exist in Greece today, the restoration of democracy can be achieved by 2 methods: either by the voluntary retirement of the present government, or by its overthrow.

"The first solution is not only without danger, but positively constructive. The 2d, which might even be brought about by uncontrolled forces, may subject the nation to new trials and tribulations.

"The government bears the responsibility for deciding, along with those who, directly or indirectly, support it.

"If, therefore, those who govern at present, captivated by power, fail to appreciate their duty, it will have to be pointed out to them by those officers who joined them in good faith. But beyond them, the whole of the country's armed forces must undertake the task. It is they who, having their origins among the mass of the people, bear the grave responsibility, on behalf of the nation, of protecting its freedom, security and independence.

"I must take this opportunity also of assuring those who are anxious about the future that I would not have broken silence if I did not believe that the country can be restored without danger to conditions of normalcy, and if I were not prepared to make my personal contribution, if need be, towards that end."

Greek Political Reaction

Panayotis Kanellopoulos, leader of the National Radical Union (ERE) and premier at the time of the coup, said in Athens "that the statement made by... Karamanlis will contribute decisively to the creation of the necessary conditions for the extrication of Greece from the impasse into which the present regime has forcibly led her. I fully share the fears expressed by Mr. Karamanlis as to the fate of the Greek nation if democracy is not speedily restored."

Constantine Mitsotakis of the Center Union party, who had been economic affairs minister under George Papandreou, said in France Oct. 2 that Karamanlis "provides a persuasive and realistic solution for the safe overthrow of the present regime in Athens and the smooth transition to a true democracy. It is also a complete answer to those who, from whatever motives, have suggested that the overthrow of the present Greek regime would result in a chaotic situation."

John Zigdis, an ex-Center Union minister, said in Athens Oct. 2 that "it is a happy event that Mr. Karamanlis, too, the former premier, declared publicly... that he intends actively to participate in the struggle for the restoration of democratic government in Greece; thus, without exception, all political leaders in the country — representing the whole nation — have taken a unanimous and unequivocal position against the present regime. This fact cannot remain without consequences."

George Mavros, ex-Center Union justice minister, said Oct. 4 in Athens that "I support every political activity tending to the return of democracy in this country. Beyond a doubt the Karamanlis statement is a very serious contribution to that action."

Anthony Brillakis, representative of the Executive Committee of the United Democratic Left (EDA) abroad, said that "the statement made by Mr. Karamanlis underlines that: the regime of the junta is today more than ever isolated even from the most conservative forces of the Greek society; the opposition of a significant part of the armed forces to the junta is gaining ground continuously; the dictatorship installed by the colonels is becoming more and more unstable mainly because of the unrelenting and total opposition of the Greek people and also because of the developing resistance movement to overthrow it."

But an EDA press release stated: "... The Greek people totally oppose the emerging anti-democratic trends observed in Mr. Karamanlis' statement, concerning the political developments after the overthrow of the junta. It is the duty of all the anti-dictatorial forces not to commit themselves to any such prospect.... The coordinated action of the resistance organizations — the Patriotic Front, the Pan-Hellenic Liberation Organization, Democratic Defense — provides a solid basis for the development of the struggle and a working solution for the mutual understanding of all the anti-dictatorial forces of the nation, so as to secure the over-throw of the junta and the victory of democracy as soon as possible."

Reaction of Underground & Resistance Groups

Andreas Papandreou, leader of the Pan-Hellenic Libera-tion Movement (PAK) resistance organization, declared in Toronto Oct. 2: "Mr. Karamanlis' statement is undoubtedly a contribution to the fight of the Greek people against the tyrannical, totalitarian regime of the colonels.... While we welcome Mr. Karamanlis' call to the armed forces to rise against the military junta, we wish to make it clear that any efforts of the military to overthrow the junta must be part of, and responsive to, the resistance effort of the Greek people as a whole....

"As far as it concerns any transition government which would take Greece to a democracy, we wish to make clear that our support is conditional upon the following: first, that the policies of the transition government express faithfully and responsibly a joint platform of the political parties and the resistance organizations. 2d, that its performance during the transition period be subject to control by an instrumentality of the parties and the resistance organizations.

"To be explicit, a transition government must guarantee: That the army, following the overthrow of the junta, will return to its barracks and serve the nation and only the nation, becoming subject to the lawfully elected civilian authority. That all the victims of the junta will be recompensed and reinstated. That all members of the junta and its chief collaborators will be prosecuted according to the law of the land. That free elections in which all parties will participate will be held within a specified period of time and that the first freely elected parliament of Greece, acting as a constituent assembly, will enact a new constitution in accordance with the will of the Greek people.

"In brief, any solution must guarantee the right of the Greek people to chart the course of their nation, and this will be the case when, and only when, the people are sovereign, the army belongs to the nation, and Greece to the Greeks."

The Patriotic Front (PAM) underground resistance organization issued from Athens a communique that was published in the underground newspaper *Nea Ellada* on Oct. 8. The communique said: PAM "welcomes Karamanlis' statement as a contribution to the struggle against tyranny. It has, however, serious reservations regarding his views on post-dictatorship procedure for the restoration of democracy and of a normal political life. At this crucial and decisive phase of the struggle we believe that . . . the best solution and one which would activate all the anti-dictatorial forces would be the formation of a 'government of national salvation.' . . . The mission of such a government would be 2-fold: To co-ordinate and direct the struggle against the dictatorship; to draw up a clear plan for the return to parliamentary democracy based on safeguarding of the fundamental democratic principle of popular sovereignty. Necessary conditions for this are: the liberation of all political prisoners; re-habilitation of the persecuted; abrogation of all junta laws and acts and of its fascist constitution, also of the emergency measures of the pre-dictatorship period; trial of the dictators; and the holding within a stated time-limit, of free elections with the participation of all parties for a parliament which would draw up the new, modern and progressive constitution of the country."

The Democratic Defense underground resistance organization said in handbills distributed in Athens Oct. 2: It welcomed "the re-entrance into the battle for the rehabilitation of Greek democracy of C. Karamanlis who, interrupting his long silence, has now demanded the ousting of the junta. Now all the healthy forces of the nation must unite their efforts so that the Greek people ... should be able to decide, by early, free and unequivocally fair elections, which form of democracy they wish to choose for themselves. We salute the initiative of Mr. Karamanlis.... We are certain that the totality of the Greek people, irrespectively of political orientation and ideology, witnessing that their liberation from the preposterous junta is now within their grasp, will unite to fight with all the means in their power the hateful dictators and bring about their downfall...."

The Freedom Front (MEL) underground group said in a press release issued in Athens: "From Sept. 30 the fight for the liberation of our country from the junta enters upon a decisive phase. Center, right and left, civilians and military, workers, employers and employees, all who suffer for the country, all who feel shame for its condition and indignation against the tyrannical actions of the junta and its accomplices, ALL GREEKS, are called to form a democratic front and to take an active part in the liberation."

The underground Communist Party (KKE) organization in Salonika circulated a proclamation, relating to the Karamanlis statement, calling on "all Communists, democrats of the Center Union and patriots of the Right" to fight "unitedly for demands and in defense of rights, to drive out the hated junta and open the way to democracy."

Foreign Reaction to Karamanlis' Statement

The *N.Y. Times* said editorially Oct. 1: "At long last the most respected and effective leader of postwar Greece has plunged wholeheartedly into the expanding effort to rid his country of a brutal and incompetent military dictatorship. Constantine Karamanlis waited a long time from his self-imposed exile in Paris to commit his enormous prestige to the fight against the colonels, but his savage, detailed indictment of them removes all doubts about where he stands." The *Times* said Oct. 6: "Washington's policy up to now has been shaped by the conviction that there is no peaceful alternative to the colonels. It has believed that encouragement of opposition might bring civil war, with the possibility of a Communist take-over and big-power involvement.... The Nixon Administration cannot ignore [the warning of Karamanlis] that entrenchment of the colonels will, in the end, not protect but rather jeopardize strategic American interests in the Mediterranean, in addition to crushing the hopes of the Greek people for freedom, decency and peace."

U.S. Rep. Donald Edwards (D., Calif.) said in an interview Oct. 26 that the timing of the Karamanlis statement "had to do with the deteriorating economic situation in Greece and the fact that the government is getting more panicky all the time, more repressive all the time.... I was very much in favor [of the statement], and it was a breath of fresh air throughout the European community. It showed again that the Greek people who are against this particular government in Greece are moderates, are conservatives; they are people who love Greece; and certainly the people who are against this junta have nothing to do with communism."

Max van der Stoel, the Council of Europe's representative on Greek affairs, said Oct. 20 before the NATO Parliamentary Assembly that the Karamanlis initiative offered an opportunity to restore freedom in Greece but that if this chance were lost, a far greater danger would remain. He acclaimed the unanimity of the Greek political world on the Karamanlis statement.

GREECE FORCED OUT OF COUNCIL OF EUROPE

Junta Announces Greek Exit from Council

Greece announced its withdrawal from membership in the Council of Europe Dec. 12, 1969 after it had become clear that at least 12 of the 18 member nations had decided to vote for a resolution, introduced by West Germany, to suspend Greece from the Council until the restoration of what the Council considered to be democratic freedoms. (The members of the Council: Great Britain, Belgium, Denmark, France, Greece, Iceland, Italy, Luxembourg, the Netherlands, Norway, Turkey, West Germany, Austria, Cyprus, Ireland, Malta, Sweden and Switzerland.)

Greek Foreign Min. Panayotis Pipinelis was instructed by the army-backed regime in Athens to announce the withdrawal after an impassioned hour-long plea to the Committee of Foreign Ministers failed to sway the nations committed to the suspension resolution. The announcement of the withdrawal denounced both the 1949 Treaty of London setting up the Council and the Convention of Human Rights. (The Council had been designed in 1949 as a political, social, and economic body reflecting the common interests of democratic countries in the Western world. Its functions are advisory, but its decisions reflect the consensus of West European views.)

Pipinelis told the committee that Greece was setting up its own democratic system and had outlined a timetable for it. Austria then called for an adjournment and lobbied for a compromise motion to postpone the decision for a few months. But an estimated minimum of 12 countries remained determined to support the suspension, and Italian Foreign Min. Aldo Moro, chairman of the committee, had, with the support of the secretariat, called for a vote requiring only a simple majority of 10 nations to pass the resolution. Pipinelis then took the floor to announce that his government had "decided to renounce Greek membership in the Council of Europe."

At a press conference following the session, Pipinelis warned that the "moral condemnation" of his government would "strengthen extremist tendencies in the country." He compared the Council's move for Greece's suspension to Russia's attitude toward Czechoslovakia; he termed it interference in Greece's internal affairs. But Pipinelis stressed that his government had no intention of leaving NATO. (The Greek government, declaring that it had won a victory, ordered flags to be flown for 3 days beginning Dec. 12.)

At a later session Dec. 12, the Council approved a unanimous resolution (Cyprus did not vote) noting the Greek withdrawal and stating that it was assumed to take effect "as from today." The resolution said that the Council:

"Considering that Greece has seriously violated the statutes of the Council of Europe, noting the situation in Greece as described . . . on Jan. 1969, noting further that the Greek government have . . . declared their withdrawal from the Council of Europe . . .;

"Understands that the Greek government will abstain from any further participation in the activities of the Council of Europe as from today;

"Concludes that on this understanding there is no need to pursue the procedure for suspension under Article 8 of the statutes;

"Charges the ministers' deputies to settle the administrative and financial consequences of this situation;

"Expresses the hope of an early return in Greece to conditions which will enable her to resume full membership of the Council of Europe."

Prior to its withdrawal from the Council, the Greek government had announced Dec. 11 that if Greece were suspended from the Council, it would have to reconsider the "value of continuing any longer her excessive contributions to European defense as well as to her efforts toward political and economic unification of Europe." The statement condemned Sweden, Denmark and Norway for their "cowardly actions"; recalled Italy's fascist past and its action against Ethiopia [in 1935]; attacked Britain and the Netherlands for their "crude colonial pasts" involving "systematic violations of human rights"; criticised Sweden for its neutrality, and said West Germany should "know the value of the role of Greece in Western defense."

Newsweek magazine reported Dec. 22 that, before the Council meeting, U.S. State Secy. William Rogers had personally pressured members of the Council of Europe not to expel Greece from the Council lest Greece retaliate by withdrawing from NATO. Rogers took this action while he was in Paris on a world tour.

George Thomson, Britain's chief delegate to the Council of Europe said Dec. 11: "If a member of a club breaks the rules for a limited period, the other members may tolerate it, but if he is in persistent violation of the rules, the time must come when the club can no longer accept the situation. My government, with great reluctance, has come to the conclusion that this is the situation we are faced with now."

Papadopoulos Bars Early Election

Premier George Papadopoulos, addressing the nation Dec. 15, said Greece had withdrawn from the Council of Europe because it could not take orders on how to run its internal affairs. He warned Greece's Western allies to beware of the threat to democracy in their own countries. In his speech, Papadopoulos ruled out the possibility of early elections in Greece and said the aims of his regime must be met first. The premier said his government would continue indefinitely to exercise all executive and legislative powers because "the people will it, because it is in their interest and because it is history's command." Papadopoulos said the government would give one year's notice before an election was held to allow time for party organization. Papadopoulos also set requirements before elections could be held. These included the reorganization of government machinery, the "cleansing of social institutions" and improvements in economic, social and political areas. He warned that "public order and security shall be preserved at the present level."

Greek Reaction to Junta's Moves

In an article published Dec. 17 in the Athens daily *Eleftheros Kosmos,* S. Constantopoulos analyzed Papadopoulos' Dec. 15 speech and derived 6 basic principles from it:

(1) Greece's commitment to total absolute sovereignty under which it would repudiate interference by any foreign power.

(2) The revolution of Apr. 1967 was not transitional. It existed in order to uproot the old institutions.

(3) The army took power to modernize Greece and to enable it to catch up with the modern world.

(4) No time-table for a return to democratic practices or elections could be set forth since this depended on conditions in Greece. Only after the revolution had fulfilled its mission could a new democracy come about.

(5) The primacy of the public interest over and above the interests of any single social class would be observed.

(6) The regime would bring about a democratic restructuring of Greek national life.

Demetrios Papaspyrou, president of the last Greek parliament, said in Athens Dec. 17 that "no nation can, in the present international circumstances, live in security and develop if it becomes isolated." Papadopoulos' Dec. 15 speech, he said, had "fully revealed the intention of the rulers to perpetuate the anomaly."

Panayotis Kanellopoulos, premier at the time of the coup and leader of the National Radical Union, said in Athens Dec. 23 that "the United States must now re-examine its whole attitude. I don't say that Washington should intervene to save us. But Washington should stop intervening in support [of the colonels]. That would be sufficient for us to find our way out."

Constantine Mitsotakis, cabinet member under the Center Union government of George Papandreou, had said in Paris Dec. 14: "The shameful defeat of the junta in the Council of Europe has put the finishing touch to the almost insane impudence of its apparent leader.... The martyred Greek people and the political leaders who speak for it feel grateful for the European assistance revealed on Dec. 12.... The Greek problem leads inevitably to the European Economic Community and NATO and to the U.S.A., which tomorrow or the next day will take final responsibility for the continuing tyranny, presents a great and contaminating danger.... The new battle which is beginning is a battle for human rights. And the politicians are bound together in their struggle to pull down the determined junta so that they may pursue these high aims: the return of Greece to the Council of Europe, participation in international organizations, the escape from gloomy isolation, the development of the rights of the people."

Andreas Papandreou, leader of the Pan-Hellenic Liberation Movement (PAK), said in Germany Dec. 13, 1969 that the silence of King Constantine in relation to the issue of the Council of Europe had caused PAK to support the permanent abolition of the Greek monarchy and the establishment of a "crownless democracy."

Foreign Reaction

Ex-Premier Jens Otto Krag of Denmark, chairman of Denmark's Social Democratic Party, said Dec. 13, 1969 that he would demand that Denmark raise the problem of Greek participation in NATO. The Copenhagen newspaper *Politiken* said Dec. 16 that Greece's withdrawal from the Council of Europe should be followed by a change in Washington's relations with Greece. *Politiken* called it "not acceptable that a regime which is not worthy of cooperating with us in the Council of Europe should have its dictatorship protected by us in NATO."

Prior to the Council of Europe meeting, the Norwegian Parliament Dec. 10 had unanimously asked its government to appeal to other NATO members not to ship military weapons to Greece.

The *Guardian* (England), in an editorial Dec. 13, said that "the Greek government should be told that members of NATO, like members of the Council of Europe, have obligations as well as rights and that a country which wants to stay in NATO must sometimes hold elections. The purposes of NATO ... include not just military security but also human liberty.... It is because the Greeks fail by that test that their future in NATO must be uncertain."

In the U.S., Rep. Donald Edwards (D., Calif.) said Dec. 12 that "the United States should recognize the stand of the Council of Europe and should support efforts to suspend Greek membership in NATO." Sen. Frank Moss (D., Utah) said Dec. 17: "The fact is that the Council [of Europe] voted to expel Greece at the end of this year on the charge that the Greek government had failed to restore democratic freedoms, and the colonels withdrew rather than face the humiliation of being kicked out.... The Council abhors the present Greek government. And furthermore, many of them feel that it is only America's apparent friendship for the regime — only our apparent support of the colonels — which keeps them in power." The *N.Y. Times* said Dec. 13: "Now the Nixon administration knows that, however the Pentagon may feel, the European allies are simply not buying the colonels' line that NATO needs Greece more than Greece needs NATO."